Social Media Marketing - Ultimate User Guide to Facebook, Instagram, YouTube, Blogging, Twitter, LinkedIn, TikTok, Pinterest

Adidas Wilson

Published by Adidas Wilson, 2020.

SOCIAL MEDIA MARKETING - ULTIMATE USER GUIDE TO FACEBOOK, INSTAGRAM, YOUTUBE, BLOGGING, TWITTER, LINKEDIN, TIKTOK, PINTEREST

First edition. September 8, 2020.

Copyright © 2020 Adidas Wilson.

ISBN: 978-1393134473

Written by Adidas Wilson.

Table of Contents

Introduction

Social media marketing, simply explained, is using social media networks to drive website traffic, increase sales and build your brand by connecting with your audience. You do this by creating great content, interacting with your followers, running ads, and analyzing the results. Currently, the main social media platforms include Snapchat, YouTube, Pinterest, LinkedIn, Twitter, Instagram, and Facebook. Initially, social media marketing involved publishing. Businesses shared content on social media hoping to generate traffic and make sales. Today, it is more than that. Businesses now use social media in many other ways. Some of those ways include social media advertising, social media analytics and social media listening and engagement. Before you start publishing content on social media, you need to come up with a social media strategy. What do you want to achieve? How can you achieve your goals using social media? Your goals may be to increase brand awareness, drive website traffic, boost sales, create a community or generate engagement. Which social platforms will work for you? instead of trying to work with all platforms, it is better to pick a few ones. Find the ones that your target audience is likely to be on. What content will you be sharing? You could share entertaining or educating content. This will depend on your marketing persona. A consistent presence is especially important, especially for small businesses. Social media is used by about three billion people. Consistency increases the chances of these people discovering your business. On social media, publishing involves sharing a video, image, or blog post. It is not different from sharing using your personal account. But with a business account, the best thing to do would be to plan, instead of posting spontaneously. It is also wise to consider the type of content you publish, when to publish it and the frequency. Make good use of scheduling tools. Conversations about your business will increase as your following grows on social media. People will privately message you, tag you on their posts and engage with your content. Other times, there will be conversations about your business without your knowledge. And you must monitor these conversations. If the conversation is negative, you can correct it before it becomes a big problem. For this purpose, find a social media listening and engagement tool. It is important to know how your strategy is performing. Are you getting more positive comments? Are more people visiting your profile and interacting with your posts? Social media platforms offer this information, but only on the basic level. There are other social media analytics tools that you can use for in-depth information. If you have funds to spare, you can use social media advertising. The ads help you reach more people, beyond your following. The advertising platforms have become so powerful—you can even choose who will see your ads. There are also advertising tools to help you manage the ads. Are you wondering what to opt for between paid and organic social media? Here is a quick answer: you may want to do both. Organic and paid social are used for different goals. If you want to balance conversion with awareness, you should know the advantages and disadvantages of both. People are using social media platforms more during the current pandemic. Ads spend, however, is not keeping up. Social media networks have reported revenue ups and downs. Many brands have paused advertising as a moral stance or because of the economic downturn. Everything is a little complicated now, but ad prices seem to be going down. So, which way should your social media marketing strategy lean? That depends on your goals. Organic Social Media includes the free content that you post on your feed—stories, memes, videos, photos, and posts. When you post, the people that will see the content are: Some of your followers (this is your organic reach). Followers' followers (when your followers share the post). If you use a hashtag, people who are following that hashtag. This may sound simple but organic social media is the best way to create a connection with your audience. It should be the foundation of every business's marketing strategy. Organic social is used to: Offer customer service. Engage customers in their buying journey. Nurture relationships. Establish a brand's voice and personality. Paid social media is advertising. Businesses pay money to social media platforms so their content can be shown to specific audiences. Paid social is used to: Drive conversions, generate leads, promote a new product, event, etc., and raise brand awareness. Paid vs organic social media has its own pros and cons. Check them out. Organic Social Media Pros - Convert new customers. Support existing customers. Establish the presence of your brand. It is free. Organic Social Media Cons takes time to get it right. Paid Social Media Pros - Reaches more people. You achieve your goals faster. You reach your target audience. Paid Social Media Cons - You need money. Requires some level of expertise. Most social media marketing strategies use organic social to engage existing customers and paid ads to attract new ones. All promotional posts do not have to be paid. A well-thought-out organic post can be just as powerful as a paid ad. Only opt for paid social if your organic social is not doing well. Promote your best organic content. If there is a post that existing customers seem to love, you can pay for new people to see it. Use A/B testing to optimize your posts. Your ads should be targeted to people who look like your organic audience. Maintain a connection with your organic audience using retargeting ads. Monitor your data to measure your results. This lets you know where you need to make changes. Make good use of automation.

Chapter 1

Managing Your Facebook Business Page

Running a Facebook business page is one of the most feasible options you can use, but a challenge to many. You need to understand the platform first to guarantee success. If you are not sure where to start, here are the ten top things you need to know beforehand. First, you need to know why you are on Facebook in the first place, what you need to get from it and whom you are targeting. Besides, you also need to understand how to achieve what you are looking for in your pursuit. Cross promotion involves linking your page to other social networks, business cards and anywhere else where you can get as many eyes online to find your business. Share your personal profile with as many people as possible and get the word out. Make sure to invest in your page if you want to get a positive result from it. Whether it is going for sponsored stories, Facebook ads, offers, promoted posts, anything that you can invest into for a positive outcome, go for it. Ensure you offer value to your visitors, along with your objective. It is advisable keeping the content valuable and worthwhile. Then promotional marketers and sponsors can see the quality you provide. One thing is that only about 16% of your fans can see your post. To change this, you can use Facebook EdgeRank to determine what post appears on your newsfeed. If you want to take the efficiency of your posts to a completely new level, then this app is for you. Apart from the EdgeRank, Facebook has other features that you can make excellent use of as well. Such features include pinned posts, featured links, post targeting highlighted posts, custom tabs, and post scheduler, to mention but a few. These features can be far reaching in effect when it comes to making your posts stand out. If you use the space offered wisely, you can create a lasting impression on your visitors and make them want to come back continuously. This applies to the cover image, the about section and the other important factors you need to address in the space offered. This section gives you the opportunity to communicate your purpose and engage your visitors. The first thing a visitor is likely to see upon landing on your Facebook page is your cover photo. As such, you need to make sure this image talks details about your business, which can help the target group associate easily with your page. If you do not post regularly, then your page's visitors are likely to stop coming back. On the contrary, posting quite often keeps the communication going and the link with your visitors alive. However, it is wise ensuring that you are posting relevant information too. Make sure you have something that builds your audience, educates them and entertainment from time to time is worthwhile. Comments may seem to be a regular thing, and quite often than not, many people do not consider responding to them. This is one area where you can build your business page to levels you could not expect. Response to comments is essential as it keeps you in touch with your visitors, and, above all, helps understand what they expect of you. Also, keep your permissions open for visitors to get in touch. It may sound easy, but it takes commitment to make your facebook business page what you want it to be. These ideas can help you get things started, just go for what works best for you. In the wake of online marketing, Facebook has been one of the avenues where you can market effectively. However, this calls for considering several things even before testing the waters. The most important barrier is competition, whether weak or strong. This can help understand reasons for failures or success on the Facebook platform. Besides this aspect, you also need to keep an eye on the following factors as well; these eight tips will take you to the top. One of the things that determine your success in Facebook is the reach you achieve with every single post. Once you post, people who have like or followed your page will see it, but this also depends on other factors as well. Above all, the best timing helps you gain an edge over the competition since others are also posting throughout the day and night. The best time to post is usually during the day when people can see what you have to offer. Not all posts perform the same, as some are more effective than others. Some of the best posts to go for include questions, videos, links, image posts, giveaways, coupons, and discounts. These posts add value but knowing what to post adds value and provides added benefit in enhancing your success. Most of the time, you need to ensure that the relevant posts on your wall are viewed by as many people as possible. In this case, posting on Sundays has been proposed as the way to go. If you are not able to post on a Sunday, Saturday is also a good day to post. How long is enough for a Facebook article? If you are using a linking strategy on Facebook to articles on your website, then you are on the right track. However, you also need to consider the length of the article you are linking too. BuzzSumo recommends using 1,000 to 2,000-word articles, as they receive more interactions than the shorter ones. Anywhere between 3,000 and 4,000 also works wonders, so that is a great option for you as well. While people will visit your page to see what you have for the day, it does not mean they come there to spend all day. This calls for shunning long descriptions and going for the shorter ones, about 50 characters at most. If you have a 10-word description, you are good to go. It is not advisable to post this type of videos on Facebook. Instead, you can opt for embedding a video or directly upload it. In case you have published a video post on your page, go a step further and upload its source on Facebook. With its versatility, Facebook works well with other social media sites; Instagram is one of these options. You can merge them so that whenever you post a picture, it is uploaded to your Facebook account. It is easier and more efficient as well. Another great tool to enhance your Facebook by boosting the engagement you get. Including hashtags in your posts can go a long way in offering results you did not expect. Ideas that can enhance your effectiveness on this platform, if well approached; this is a great way of enhancing your Facebook marketing.

Chapter 2

Make Your Facebook Post Command Attention

Once you have your Facebook page up and ready, what you post there is as important as the page itself. Therefore, you have to go an extra mile to ensure you have the right posts that will keep your visitors coming back for more every day. This means knowing what your business audience needs and what the clients are expecting of you. Whenever you are posting on your page, you should ensure you have a clear objective behind the necessity to communicate. Start by analyzing what you want to get from a post, as this is reliable in making it more efficient. Remember, the goal of your post should be apparent. There are many ways you can use a post to engage your visitors. You can ask a question, or post a photo and let them caption, leave a blank for them to fill in and many other ways as well. The best thing here is to draw them closer. Just make it short, but ensure it is compelling enough. Using a concise yet compelling language and or image, but keep vague or deceptive language at bay, if you want to generate clicks, a little professionalism can work out best for you. Posting photos have been known to receive more attention over word posts but posting a link has been found to outperform the photos. Therefore, combining both a photo post and link can be more efficient. Just ensure that the page where the link leads has a big picture that will appear along with a short description of the post. If this is not the case, then you can just paste a photo and a brief link to go with it. One of the things your visitors will keep coming back is if they find inspiration in your posts. As such, this aspect is one of the essential things you cannot afford to leave out in your post. All you need to do here is ensure your sentiments are authentic enough. You can use memes, quotes that your audience can relate with and inspirational photos if you want to enhance shares. An excellent post does not have to be promotional always. Your Facebook is not an advertisement billboard. Therefore, although you will need to do promotions and offers from time to time, it is wise to ensure you are not over doing it. Consider providing helpful content for your audience apart from just promotions. Going for a mixture of the two can go a long way in making things work out best. A well-crafted post can attract visitors and keep the existing followers. It is thus advisable to utilize the effectiveness of this factor to ensure you make the best out of every single post. Make every post count.

Chapter 3
Running Your Facebook Business Page

Most of the time, people do not take Facebook business pages as seriously as they should. As a result, many end up making mistakes that cost them negative effects and reviews. If you are running a business page on this platform, then ensure you keep these mistakes at bay. Making it about you - This is the first misconception. Many think that their business page on Facebook is about them, but the opposite is the case. This page should be more about your visitors; you should keep them in mind and only post about yourself occasionally. One of the things you need to avoid is making your page boring by posting almost every other minute. No matter how great your posts are, just posting in a one out of ten ration goes a long way in communicating to your visitors. You do not have to flood them with dame information repeatedly to let them know what you have, just take it slow. Running a dormant page is a mistake that goes unnoticed and can be devastating. If you are not ready to manage the page, do not start it until you are sure you are capable of posting continually. This means ensuring you post regularly, not just once a month and you disappear. You are not social - The word speaks volumes; social media is about being social. If you fail in this aspect, then you have just lost. Being social includes keeping in touch with your visitors by giving them content, engaging them and responding to their comment too. Maintain the connection, and you will have engaging eyes coming back for more. The Facebook business page cannot efficiently perform if you do not link it appropriately. You need to ensure you keep it connected to other sources where visitors can get detailed information on some matters. Keeping your page locked out of the outside world will only do it more harm than good. The perception your visitor will have about you and your business depends on the first impression they get from you. This relies on the cover image you put on your page. If the photo does not positively or concisely represent your business, then you may lose potential customers or readers. Lack of proper timing to get your audience can cost you. You need to analyze your prospective visitors and identify the best time they are likely to see your posts. This helps earn a level of certainty that your point is getting to the intended audience. It is advisable that you post during weekends, especially if you are targeting consumers. This being a business page does not mean you go in with a clenched formal approach. This will likely be perceived as inaccessible, which can dent your connection with visitors. It is wise you post slowly on the professional approach and embrace a personality approach so that others can relate to you easily. These mistakes may appear ineffective, but they can be devastating if two or more affect your business page. Therefore, you need to ensure you keep them in check to keep your page's performance at its best. Creating a Facebook page is one thing but making it a successful one is another thing altogether. If you are looking to make your page stand out, then you need to include these four simple steps. One essential thing to keep an eye on here is your ideal client. The idea behind knowing your prospective visitors helps utilize your space well to put the right information in the right section, where it can be clearly seen. Going for niche marketing and segmentation is also far reaching in page success, as this enhances focusing on your target audience. Remember, the more you narrow down, the better. If you want to make your page look like a website you brought right into Facebook, then the way you brand is the secret. This helps you bridge Facebook to your sites, although you do not have to rush your clients through Facebook. Avoid creating more clicks for your visitors to get to your site, as this may work against what you intended to achieve. If there is one formula that is usually underrated by most business owners, then it is inbound marketing. The fact is that marketing tactics are essential for the success of any intention to bring traffic to your doorstep, and Facebook is no different. Primarily, this strategy has to do with using keywords, videos, opt-in opportunities as well as cross-promotions. You need to ensure you have great content on your FB page as you would with a website or blog. The good news is that there are apps like Networked Blog that you can use to link this content and beef up your Facebook page. The best thing you can do for your page is to be committed efficiently, and this means real-time engagement. This means taking action whenever necessary for time and effort to materialize. As such, you need to keep coming back to your page and check out the interests, likes, opinions from your visitors and other important things. The best thing to remember here is the fact that engagement is all about doing it for your fans than for yourself. To achieve this, ensure your posts are more about your fans and give them an opportunity to talk about themselves. Coming up with a successful Facebook page is never the easiest thing to do, but it does not have to freak you out nevertheless. Knowing what to do and why you need to have it done is the first step in realizing this essential aspect. Therefore, understanding what is expected of you can go a long way in preparing you to tackle the task efficiently. This can necessitate checking out other Facebook pages to get an idea of what you need to do. After that, commitment and sacrificing your time to tend to your page comes in handy. Above all, remember to make it more about your fans than yourself. Not all pages are successful; the following is a list of pointers to run a Facebook page effectively. Name - Pick out a name that stands out; name that most users are likely to use while searching for the product. URL - Pick out a URL that is easy for your customers to remember and write. Description - Update the about section below the cover photo. Make use of hyperlinks to give a detailed description of your products and location. Optimize the search engine result - Use keywords that are easily identifiable in the Google search engines.

Strategize - Design a plan of activities and develop long-term goals of the Facebook Page. Develop a content calendar - Create some activities and the dates you would like to accomplish them on your Facebook page. Cover photo - The photo appearing as your cover photo should speak vividly on the kind of business you run. Regularly Posting - Make relevant posts on the Facebook page on a regular basis. Respond to comments - Ensure you revert on all posts as soon as you can. Administration - Do not manage the page alone, make other people co-administrators. Accessibility - Fill in the contact details section so that people can get you even if you are offline. Look at the analytics. - Constantly look for the customer satisfaction with your products and check on any new trends. Profile Photo - Create a photo that will lead people into knowing more about you. Invite friends to like the page - Through the tagging Facebook feature, you can easily invite your Facebook friends to like your page. Ensure you market your Facebook page across other social media platforms such as Twitter and Whatsapp. Allow the fans to message you concerning the products directly. Check out for the Facebook insights on the kind of content the followers would easily engage with. Do not merely type or share another status, include pictures and videos as part of the content. Be brief on your posts. Most people will not read through lengthy posts. Put up posts that solicit nice responses from fans, starting with words like what do you think about our product? Consider your audience before using specific kind of tone. Ensure you are not left out on the latest online trends. Allow promotional advertisements on your page to create revenue. Promote products of other pages through tagging them. In this manner, you gain more fans. Pinning a post ensures that all members will get to reading the post. Create a post then schedule the time it will be posted to reach a larger audience. Run several contests and reward the participants. Make sales through an online purchase made through Facebook posts. Select the targeted audience through posting at times The tips in this chapter will ensure that your Facebook page remains active and that you gain more followers online.

Chapter 4
Video Marketing on Facebook

Over the years, Facebook has evolved into paving the way to video ads. Thanks to its creative and market-oriented developers. You can use the following tips to jump-start your marketing with video ads, taking advantage of the new and revolutionary Facebook feature. When making a Facebook video make sure to be driven by your target audience. Know the products and services they like and are likely to buy. Here you have the advantage of a huge client base that will instantly want to be a part of the buying team once they see you have them in mind and give them what they want. Be sure to come up with something they will look forward to. One thing you must know about Facebook is that it is not a place for serious ads. Hey, don't make serious videos, entertain your customers too. This is a simple remedy that will keep them hooked and look forward to your videos, products, and services. All work and no play make Jack a dull boy. Be careful not to make your customers dull. Are your videos pinned? You need to get your videos pinned. A powerful tool that gives you the freedom to 'stick' your videos at the top of your page; it is simply glued there. Why? To make the videos easily visible and noted, it is guaranteed to be the first post to be seen. A pinned video cannot be pushed anywhere even when you are publishing new content. Do you know why the novel Dear John by Nicholas Sparks was adapted into a movie? Of course you do, people are enticed with watching rather than reading. Movie's only taken 1 hour and 30 minutes to watch whereas the novel may take you weeks and weeks of reading. Because people prefer videos why don't you make more and more to emphasize the importance of your products and services and how they can get them? Adding more high-quality videos is multiplying your fan base. Is your video making sense? Don't bother begging to be followed or shared. You may annoy potential fans and followers. Instead, create a meaningful message, one that can easily be understood by your target audience. For instance, create a very short video with the intended message then link the audience to your blog for more information about deals, coupons, and discounts. Also, make sure your video is interactive. Facebook Power Editor is a powerful tool when correctly used as it may yield a good number of new consumers. It is used to create and post videos. To make it notable, the ads are placed in the newsfeed, helping in notifying your user about the video. In other words, be consistent with your message and keep posting new videos regularly. However, make sure the videos are high-quality, interesting, entertaining, and straight to the message. Thanks to Facebook, marketing your products are easier. Go ahead and make your customers want your products through watching your captivating and informed video content. Facebook is amongst the fastest growing social media platforms. The growth is in terms of an increase in the number of subscribers having Facebook profiles. As such, Facebook is a great site for marketing your business. Despite the strategic Facebook marketing platform, some businesses struggle to effectively carry out marketing on Facebook. Here are some tips on successful marketing of your Facebook page. Currently, there are a huge number of business pages on Facebook. Ensure that your Facebook page stands out among others. Ensure the cover and profile photo reflects the kind of business activities you are engaged in. The description section should give details of the products and provide business contacts. Choose a descriptive and memorable username. Select a vanity universal resource locator that users will easily remember. The Facebook page address will be based on your username. Choose a username that reflects the kind of business activity that you are engaged in. However, your business page should have at least twenty-five likes to claim a vanity URL. The about section provides an opportunity of using text-based keywords. Ensure that the keywords can help customers in the identification of the page. It helps when someone searches for queries; Facebook directs them to your page. Also, include your URL in the description section. Facebook allows for one pinned post per group. Make the most use of the post; ensures it is attractive and communicates about your products to potential customers. Ensure you have selected the appropriate business category. Select the best category for your business such as local business and indicate the region covered. It helps customers in their searches to easily identify your age. Different customers may log into their accounts at various times. Schedule your postings on a weekly basis. Each post should carry key details on any updates on business products. You can schedule the time that your post appears on the Facebook page to create consistency. Enrich the content of your Facebook page posts. Facebook allows for more than just a text post. Use images and videos to make the Facebook content interesting. Use Hyperlinks to connect users to descriptive information on the products and services on the page. Encouraging social sharing on your page. To optimize on the number of people of people who get to view your Facebook posts enable the sharing and liking features. In this manner, users can get to share your post with their Facebook friends. It increases the customer base. Facebook advertisements are a great way in which you can promote your business. Alongside your advertisement, there should be a link leading people to your page. However, Facebook advertisements are paid for. Use the advertisements strategically to profit your business. The tips mentioned are a great way of boosting your Facebook page. Use each tip creatively to attract more fans which means more sales for your products. Facebook Video live is the new feature on the social media site. It brings forth numerous opportunities for business users to connect live, and increase the sale of goods and services. Here are some ways in which someone can use the Facebook live Video for business; Discussing a topic on the blog post that you have previously posted is a great boost for your business. Even though you can answer your users' comments on Facebook live, it is better if you can schedule the live session so as to address each question as it comes forth. The users' can either replay the session or watch it live. The Facebook live video is an excellent way of looking into your business through offering behind the scenes pictures. You can share the process of getting into your line of work with the users. Facebook live is a keyway of promoting an upcoming event in your business. After the preparations for the event are over, schedule a time to make a special live video on the same. During the announcement of the event ensure you have a universal resource locator that your fans can easily remember. Post the link in the video comments section for users. During the actual event, stream live on Facebook for users who might have missed attending the event. Before you bring in the actual products on the shop, give the viewers a sneak peek into the new arrivals. Consider putting a link to the Live Video to take preorders; maximize on the customers' excitement on the new product. Use the Facebook live video to answer customers' questions about your business products. Customer service is an integral part of entrepreneurial activities. Ensure you answer all questions that come your way, even if it is repeated questions; this may be time-consuming. Live videos provide an opportunity for looking into some of the most asked questions in one instance. The customer service team may help in identification of some common questions. A customer can replay the sessions later. You can create a Facebook note so that all team members can access the video. Engage with Facebook live group members. Apart from running a Facebook page, you might have a Facebook group where you interact with users. You can have weekly updates of your products and services. If you run more than one Facebook group, this is a great way of connecting members to a variety of services offered. Live group broadcasts provide an opportunity for deepening your relationships with people. Custom settings on the Facebook group, so that you can be the only one making such a live video on the group. Invest in additional voice boosting equipment to ensure audibility. Facebook Video Live is a great way of ensuring customers gets a vivid description of the business and its products. It gives a chance of real-time interactivity that boosts connection between the seller and the potential buyers.

Chapter 5
Facebook for Marketing

Facebook is the leading social media site with many users who daily log into their counts. People connect with their friends' online and share on the life progress on various issues. Facebook marketing is a new trend where people purchase items from advertised Facebook posts. The following are ways in which one can market items online on Facebook; There are no fees charged for creating a Facebook account. A Facebook page enables a business to identify itself through sharing images, links, and posts. A customized Facebook page gives customers a better grasp of the kind services and goods offered. Unlike Facebook accounts, pages do not have a limitation on the number of friends. Additionally someone does not have to be your friend to like your posts. Online marketing can efficiently be as simple as placing advertisements on a Facebook page. The advertisements come on the side of a Facebook page. It includes a picture of the item on sale in addition to the link or hyperlink to a business page. You can customize each advertisement to meet a specific group of users or for a certain location. Holding various Facebook contests on items and rewarding participants is a great awareness creation tool. Many people get to know your brands through such contests. The contests will direct users in participation on a third party already established application. Sponsored stories are a kind of advertisement where a user gets to share the experience with the certain product. If someone went for snacks at MacDonald's their friends can easily get to learn of their experience. In this way, products are promoted and get more users. Sponsored stories are the only advertisement available on the mobile devices. Once a user likes a certain business page, the information is automatically posted on the newsfeed. A brand gets more fans through sponsored stories. Unlike the other advertisement tools where one just likes or comments on a specific story; an open graph creates interactivity between the users and the seller. The third party application enables the actions that users perform on Facebook posts. Entrepreneurs need creativity in deciding the kind of action users can take such as listen or read. Retailers get the chance of placing real-time bidding. Through the exchange tool, a retailer can create re-advertise a post when a retailer visits and fails to make a purchase. The advertisements used to appear in the side column but currently appear on the newsfeed. These tools are great in carrying out marketing on the Facebook site. Through these tools, a business gains the much-needed publicity. Facebook Ad's - All social media platforms provide an opportunity for creating advertisements. Still, Facebook is the best site in terms of features, insights, and audience. Facebook is an ideal place for a business to start from. Many businesses end up misusing their resources when Facebook ads become ineffective. It is vital to have knowledge of the manner in which Facebook works and its best practices. Here are some tips for creating a successful Facebook Ad. Facebook offers insights into the kind of business that generates revenues and best-selling products. The insights are integral in the determination of whether a product is worth the effort. The publisher will learn the specifics on a particular audience before spending money while targeting them. The Facebook insights work through mining data from the people who have liked your Facebook page and showing their preferences on your products. It saves time and money on advertising according to customer's desires. Create Unique Advertisement sets for each audience. Every audience is unique, especially when dealing with a variety of products. You can select two advertisements or more depending on your targeted audience. Still, the same ad can be sent to two different audiences. For example, when dealing with clothing, you can target individual persons as well as entrepreneurs who will consider buying in bulk. Put landing pages in each advertisement. Before placing the Facebook, advertisements ensure that you have a business Facebook page. It allows users to be familiarized with your product before placing in any marketing tactic. Also, Facebook advertisements allow hyperlinking. The advert should lead people to the page to learn more on the product. Before placing any advertisement, ensure there are likes on your Facebook page. This way, you will not spend money on an advertisement without a set clientele that you are targeting. Striking advertisements are important for drawing attention to your Facebook ad. Many people major in how to create the advertisement with no mention of the image. Visual attraction is important. Hire an expert to create the advertisement if you cannot do it. Facebook indicates that you cannot use images that contain more than twenty words. Limit the text used. Images will attract attention to your advertisement. Before developing an advertisement setup, a bid strategy. A budget is needful to avoid overspending. Optimized CPM allows you to put together a budget and strategy. This tool develops an advertisement based on the constraints and goals provided. Until you are well versed with the cost of space on Facebook, let Facebook develop the advertisement for you to minimize overspending. Creation of a killer Facebook advertisement is based on understanding the platform and maximizing on the features. As much as the advertisement is important, the platform used is important. Create a Facebook page and build on it. Still, keep in mind that technology is changing. Familiarize yourself with changing features. Facebook with almost a billion users provides a perfect platform for conducting business. Despite its potential, not all Facebook business markets effectively manage to create revenue. Strategy is important. Consider the kind of business you are starting, look into ways of attracting attention, conversion channels and getting the customers to purchase your products. The Following steps are important in Facebook revenue generation; Marketing is one way in which someone can get money on the Facebook platform. Also take advantage of the Facebook ads to lead clickers to a particular site. You can sell the advertisements to website owners to increase the clientele base. Once customers get directed to websites, they can easily purchase products sold there. Additionally, Website owners will make a profit. It entails selling to fans through posting from your Facebook page directly into Facebook newsfeed. Fans may be more responsive when acquired through ads than through contests. However, you need to be more creative to attract and maintain the fan numbers. Most companies have an e-mail where they can easily get the required fans support. Through the emails, companies get to market their products through the thousands of subscribers. This is a profitable endeavor. Facebook advertisements can additionally be profitable for business activities through additional fan numbers. Facebook advertisements can get mailed to subscribers depending on different criteria's such as; age, gender, location, interests, relationship status, workplace, and education levels. Add the qualified target group and send the email to the subscribers. An integration of ads and email can lead to increased sales in a company. Many business marketing tactics are yet to incorporate texting as a tool for generating revenue. One needs to create a Facebook advertisement, reach out to fans, and allow fans to share their contacts. Once you get the contacts, send discounted sale text messages. A good percentage of the fans will respond through making purchases. The Shop revenue will increase. Increase Traffic to your Ad supported site. You can start through the creation of a Facebook page. Increase number of likes through making scheduled posts containing images and texts. After increasing the fans number on your Facebook business page, post a link every time there is an article in your ad supported site. The new page views from new readers' means additional revenue for your website. The Five models are proven for incoming generating activities. However, there are some methods which are complicated for beginners. It is advisable to start up with simple Facebook advertisements. The ads help in increasing traffic for the sale of your products. Facebook ads are a great way of acquiring fans. Consider the creativity and amount of time required in running the application before beginning. Unskilled advertisement leads to minimal interaction between the customers and the sellers. Most people use social media platforms for connecting with their friends. Did you know that Facebook generates a lot of money? During the first quarter of 2017, Facebook generated a whopping $7.01 Billion. Still, marketers use other social media platforms in making money. Here, we are going to show you ways in which you can make money with your Facebook account, from creating advertisements, custom making fan pages and the creation of applications. Facebook Shop has two versions free and paid applications. Create an e-store where you can sell your products. Basically, you will own a store on Facebook. Café Express created Magic moments to enable users to take a picture or a video of their products and effectively sell them online. The platform is mainly for artistic work such as customized mugs. The garage sale is an application connected to buy. Com. It enables someone to sell used items and make extra money virtually. Zazzle application has got a neat feature "my merch store." You can use it to sell items through connecting it to your Facebook page. You can promote your eBay listing on Facebook and make sales. The easy social shop is a free application. It enables one to import all your products from the application store to your Facebook page. Once the product is on the Facebook page, you can market it to millions of Facebook users. People think of eBay as the only online shopping place. However, you can still sell your products on the Facebook marketplace. The products may vary from baby items, toys, and even furniture. Links are an important way of informing family and friends on the items you are selling. However, do not send multiple links that make people suspect it for scamming. Affiliate marketing requires that you sign up on a marketing site such as Purchase junction. Search the marketplace for a product to promote. Acquire your distinct link for marketing and then share it with your contacts on Facebook. Not all people are techno-savvy. People still rely on e-books to guide them. Consider publishing a book on how to use Facebook or any other interesting title. Create a Facebook blog and update it on a daily or a weekly basis. On the blog, you could run advertisements or offer services such as custom making fan pages. In this way, you will earn revenue. Develop your own Facebook Application. If you can code, an application is a great way of earning revenue. The app features will help users, and you can sell it. Do sponsored Likes and shares. People like and share posts to earn income. If you are an expert in marketing, you can sell your skills to earn income. Sites like Fiverr allow anyone to place a gig and sell their likes or shares on a specific Facebook page. Create Unique Fan pages and sell them to customers. The fifteen strategies enable one to choose the best way to earn money online. Also, there is a variety of options if one method fails.

Chapter 6
Secrets to Facebook Success

Facebook is one of the leading social media sites globally with over 1.28 billion users who log into it daily. Mark Zuckerberg one of the Facebook co-founders is deemed to be among the most successful people. He realized some of the top secrets in establishing a growing social media site. Here are some of the secrets of Facebook success; Zuckerberg did not have a business plan on Facebook. He simply built the application software during his free time at Harvard. He did not seek advice from business people and his friends; he simply implemented his project. Unlike most of the entrepreneurs who conduct a market research for their products, Zuckerberg built the Facebook application and launched it on the market. Since the inception of Facebook, there was a legal fight on whom the real owner of Facebook is. Two Harvard seniors claimed that Zuckerberg had stolen their application. Ideas need to be executed. The infrastructure used to build Facebook is simple. Instead of sophisticated products that take a lot of time to grow, build a simple product, and it will function in the shortest time possible. With the growth in access to the internet worldwide, there was no product like Facebook in existence. Zuckerberg created a new product. Twitter at some point competed with Facebook on popularity. However, Facebook prevailed since there are few pseudo accounts as people use their real names, unlike handles. One thing that could bring Facebook down is its infrastructure. Several social media sites had sprung but failed in holding the user's population. Zuckerberg started by adding small groups of people until he was certain Facebook could manage multiple registrations. Despite the income generated through advertisement on Facebook, Zuckerberg has focused on the Facebook sole purpose, socialization. The strength of Facebook lay in the great team of workers. A good company depends on the kind of people that are hired and fired. Any successful company must maintain the control of customers, employees, and shareholders. There should be a balance of the interests of these three groups of people. From the beginning, Zuckerberg was the CEO of Facebook despite having poor leadership qualities. Later, he built a team of advisors who helped him develop CEO qualities. Not all critics are healthy for business development. Learn to put up with the people's critics. Zuckerberg was criticized for being a bad leader. It never derailed his quest for growth and advancing in his passion. Ignore most of the would-be partners and deal markers. Some people are out to make an impact through a change of your agenda. Ignore the input that can take you off your vision. However, look out for potential business partners. The main goal of any business idea is crucial. Despite the up and downs during the business developmental stages, focus on the goal for many decades. The thirteen secrets helped Zuckerberg build a strong team of workers. With Zuckerberg as the CEO, Facebook value continues to grow as it serves its core purpose of connecting people.

Chapter 7
How to Make Money with Your Blog

At first, blogging used to be a personal web log where someone would write about their day. "Blog" came from the term "web log". Some entrepreneurs saw that having a blog opened a marketing opportunity and that is how blogging took off. Apart from marketing, a blog can also be a business. There are numerous people who have no idea what the difference between a blog and a website is. This can be partly attributed to the fact that most enterprises use both and merge them into one web presence. However, a blog is not like a traditional website and there are two of its features that prove this: Blogs require to be updated frequently. New content in a blog is added a few times a week. Blogs engage the reader. They usually have a comment section where readers can interact with the blogger and other readers. Entrepreneurs have resorted to blogging for several reasons: Search engines favor new content. Blogging is a useful tool for SEO (search engine optimization). Blogging lets you keep your clients and customers updated on what is happening with your business; you can tell them about any new deals and offer them tips. With a blog you can nurture rapport and trust with your potential customers. As you show off how knowledgeable you are, you build credibility. Blogs can be a source of income. There are many ways through which you can make money from your blog such as affiliate products and advertising. Blogging is portable and flexible, making it perfect for lifestyle entrepreneurs. Blogging is a source of income and a powerful marketing tool—that is what makes it popular. However, it is not all unicorns and rainbows. Before you decide that blogging is for you, consider the downsides below: Blogging can be time consuming. You must update it regularly for it to be engaging to readers and effective at SEO. You need to have ideas if you want to write regularly. Nonetheless, you can hire freelancers or allow guest writers. There is another option of buying PLR (private label right) content and tweaking it to suit your post. You will not see immediate results. Initially, you will not make as much. You must build momentum and readership. Blogs are affordable and easy to start. You only need to follow these simple steps: Set up the blog: you can choose a free option (Blogger or WordPress) but it is best to invest in hosting and a domain name. Add content: have a schedule for creating and posting articles. A content calendar would be helpful. Market: marketing will contribute to the success of your blog. Find a way to reach your target market either through an email list, social media, or other bloggers. Add income streams: try out affiliate marketing or feed ad networks like Google AdSense.

Everyone needs some extra cash. People often say that blogging is an easy way of making money. But how do you do this? Once you have set up the blog, what next? Your blog is not a get-rich-quick scheme. But it is a good way of making money. Read on to find out how. Monetize with CPM or CPC Ads - Placing ads on a website is the most common mode of making money for bloggers. Most ads fall into one of two popular categories: CPC/PPC ads: pay per click or cost per click ads are in form of banners placed on your sidebar or in your content. You get paid every time a visitor clicks on the ad. CPM ads: these are "cost per 1000 impressions" ads. You are paid a fixed a fixed amount depending on the number of people that view the ad. Google AdSense is the most well-known program for these kinds of ads. Others include Media.net, Infolinks, and Chitika. When it comes to placing ads, you do not have to work with advertising programs. If your blog receives a lot of traffic, advertisers will start reaching out to you asking you to sell ads. You can also find the advertisers yourself. This is better than using networks because you get to cut out the middleman. This is how affiliate marketing works: A seller or advertiser wants to sell a product. The two of you agree that if you help them sell it, you will get a commission. You are given a unique link (it will be used to track your affiliate code). You then place the link on your site. If someone clicks through and buys the product, you get a percentage of the full price. Amazon Associates is a good place to start. Selling your own digital products is also another great idea. The products can include: Themes, Plugins, Apps, Music, Video, Images, Online courses, and eBooks. Before you get into this, make sure your readers need the product. Do not just assume. It is wise to know and understand your visitors first, then make a product that solves their problem. You can make money by selling physical products as well. This involves using your blog for content marketing and drive readers to your actual business website. Sell anything from manufactured products to handmade goods. Another way of making money is by selling memberships to special areas of your website. If you have a career blog, for instance, you could charge a monthly fee for readers to access your job board. The exclusive membership must be something valuable. Do not sell a service that they can get for free elsewhere. If your blog is popular and the content is great, people will recognize you as a guru in the niche (whatever you are blogging on). People may then start approaching you for opportunities in the industry.

Chapter 8
How to Find a Blogging Niche

B efore you start your new blog, you need to find a niche. Going Too Broad one of the most common mistakes that beginners make—going for a broad niche. Many times, people fear to go too narrow when starting out. They believe that if their focus is broad, they will attract more visitors. However, that is not true. If your niche is too broad, you will have a hard time pulling search engine traffic. Here is what may make a beginner give up: They choose a broad topic. It fails to gain traction with search engines. The beginner is discouraged and gives up. If you choose a narrow topic, you will soon become an expert. Google uses the Hummingbird algorithm which gives an advantage to websites that cover a topic well. A smaller field has less topics to cover and less competition. Humans, just like search engines, love narrow niches. If they find specifically what they are looking for, they will establish a strong bond with your site. What Exactly Is a Blogging Niche? It is a niche that attracts a subset of a larger market. Check out these examples: Travel > Frugal Travel, Gardening > Cold Climate Gardening, Fitness > Fitness for Nerds. An online research tool is useful when it comes to getting niche ideas. An example is the Keyword Niche Finder by Wordstream. You get the first 30 searches free. Key in your head or main keyword and explore the longtail variations. See if there is a niche you like. Finding a Blogging Niche – Passion. Experts recommend getting a niche that is at the intersection of revenue potential and your passion. Others say that if you want to earn a living with blogging, you should focus more on profits. Nonetheless, finding a topic you love is important because it will show in your writing and you will stay motivated. Finding a Niche – Profitability. A keyword research will help you determine the profitability of your niche. Find a paid keyword research tool that has cost per clicks (CPC) among its metrics. Enter about 10 keywords in your niche. If the keywords' CPC is a few dollars, it is a profitable niche. In case you cannot get a keyword research tool: Browse a newsagent's magazine stand. If you see a magazine for your niche, then it is profitable. Publishing is expensive. Enter your keyword in the Google search box. If you see paid ads, the niche has money. Type a few keywords on Amazon. For each review, there are 1000 customers. Find best blogs and affiliate programs in your niche using Google. For keyword research, you need to assess: Overall trends – use Google Trends (it is free), Keyword competition, Search volume. For the last two, you will need a paid tool such as KWFinder, Keyword Tool Pro, Spyfu, SEMrush, Ahrefs etc. For competition and volume, you can also use: Rand Fishkin's Method and Brian Clark's Method. The word "copywriting" gets thrown around so much that it is slowly losing its meaning. Many people have no idea what it is anymore. So, here is a deeper look at the term. There are tons of jobs that fall under the category of copywriting. It is no wonder that even copywriters find it hard to explain their own job. Ask one and note how they dance around the definition. This is the same case with Dictionary.com. They barely define the word. "A writer of a copy" is not much of a definition. Towards the end, the explanation tries to be a little more specific with "especially for advertisements or publicity releases". The best explanation you will find is a comparison between content writing and copywriting. The latter is said to inform readers while the former calls them to action. This is a good place to start. Creation of valuable and relevant content is required for both content writing and copywriting. The difference, therefore, must be in the engagement potential. Going by this, copywriting can be defined as a way of writing that is engaging, strategic and actionable. What is the relationship between copywriting and advertisement? How does it fit into marketing? Traditional advertising is barely surviving. It is not dead, yet, but it is not doing well either. Audiences do not care about paid commercials anymore. They respond better to organic marketing (both outbound and inbound). Every marketing campaign starts with copywriting. Internet users get information for what they want to buy from search engines. Copywriters encourage these shopping instincts using engaging wording and alluring themes. It is a win-win situation. Brands rank better in search engines and readers benefit from relevant, entertaining information. Copywriters must know how to play with words, obviously. But there is more. Beyond writing: other than basic writing skills, a copywriter should have immaculate grammar, a broad vocabulary and unique writing style. Resourcefulness: most copywriters, especially beginners, must write about a lot of topics. This means being able to find trustworthy and relevant resources. Creativity: even with technical topics, a copywriter should find a way to make the content engaging. Reader-centricity: SEO is not really a copywriter's job, but they must be knowledgeable about it. Regardless of what a copywriter is writing about, they first must think about how to entice a reader in every step. Niche and Market Research involves familiarizing yourself with the needs and expectations of the reader. Knowing what motivates their purchase decision helps you create content that resonates with them. A reader should clearly see the benefits they will get in your content. There are three equally valid principles that contribute to valuable content. AIDA: A – attention I – interest D – desire A – action. You vs. We: focus on the reader's needs. When you have done your research properly, content creation will be a walk in the park. Pen down all the information you have gathered to make a raw copy. Read and re-read the copy. Polish the grammar, tone, and any other issue to come up with the perfect copy, ready for publishing. Having a full-time professional blog costs more than just your time. Here is how much you may have to pay (these are the minimum costs). Laptop: a desktop computer is good, but a laptop is better because you can work from anywhere. Other than a HD screen and a long battery life, the minimum requirements are an i5 processor and 8GB RAM. Cost: $2399 for Apple and $679 for PC. Microphone and webcam: at some point, people will want to see the face behind the content. A good webcam and microphone will help you make quality vlogs. Cost: $170. DSLR and lenses: amazing photos will capture the attention of your audience. Cost: $450. When it comes to hosting companies, you have a lot of options to choose from. Make sure you choose a reliable company. Otherwise, you will have to deal with poor customer support, unending downtimes, and a lot of other inconveniences. Cost: $2 to $20/month. Both your blog name and domain name are part of your brand identity. Your blog will appear more professional and boost credibility. You can buy the domain name either from a hosting company or a registrar. Cost: $14/ year. Depending on how much money you have, you can choose to: Have professionals create a custom design for you, tailored to meet the unique needs of your blog. Buy a common WordPress theme. Use the services of a freelancer or company. The WordPress theme is the cheapest option ($30 - $60). Highly customized professional blogs can cost up to $2500 or even more. Growing your blog organically will take time. You can start by posting high-quality articles every week. If you do not have the time, find a freelance copywriter to do the work for you. they charge from $15 to about $50 an hour. This is a good idea for pure blog sites. However, for business sites with a blog section, it is better to pay for content instead of having a full-time copywriter. As your website grows, you will start getting offers from writers wanting to contribute. Before you accept the offers, check the links and content to ensure that everything is in line with your brand. Beginner bloggers can opt for free advertising methods which will only cost their time. Professionals, on the other hand, should consider paying for promotion and advertising. Google have a service, Google AdWords, that you can use to promote on Google Search. They do not charge to display your link. You only pay when someone clicks on the link ($1 to $50). They allow you to pause, stop and start the campaign whenever you like. Other forms of advertising include LinkedIn, Twitter, and Facebook ads. Facebook advertising is great because you get to reach your target audience. Most of the software tools you will need are free such as Google Docs. You may need the services of a speech recognition tool sometime in the future. There are also writing and management tools. To fine-tune content, you may need a software to check grammar mistakes and/or plagiarism.

Chapter 9
How to Increase Blog Traffic

Increasing blog traffic is one of the most challenging things about having a blog. Hopefully, these tips will help. Tailor your content for a specific audience. Use catchy headlines for more clicks. Make your content easy to read. Create long-form, evergreen content. Try user-generated content. Blog consistently— work with a schedule. Create SEO-friendly content. Conduct proper keyword research before writing. Have an appealing website design. Make the site responsive (on every device). Let your content include visuals. Be wise while naming images (keyword instead of random letters). Your images should have a description. Occasionally share funny content on social media (it does not have to be related to your blog). Interlink content so people can read more articles on your site. Create social share buttons. Have your site's link on your social media profiles. Interact with people on Q&A websites. Comment on other people's blogs. Invite your readers to comment on posts. Ask family and friends to share your blog. Interact with fellow bloggers and share your blog with their audience. Get people to subscribe to your blog. Write guest posts on other sites. Allow other bloggers to guest post on your site. Attend networking events and conferences. Collaborate with fellow bloggers. Organize your own events—local or online. Track your numbers using Google Analytics. Make use of Twitter. Mention businesses or people in your tweets. Make use of Facebook. Create a page for your blog. Get into Facebook groups. Make use of Google+. Get into Google+ communities. Make use of Reddit. Try the Reddit advertising program. Share content on Imgur. Make use of Instagram. Share your content on

Pinterest. Reshare old posts on social networks. Do not forget
LinkedIn. Join Mix (formerly StumbleUpon). Submit your posts to
Mix. Join ViralContentBee. Get more followers on Twitter with
Tweepi. Share content automatically with Buffer. Post videos on
YouTube. Get your blog featured on Alltop. Add your site to
Blogarama. Join forums. Get into a blogging community. Try a
giveaway. Add your articles to Wikipedia as resources. Create a
Wikipedia page of your own. Write roundups. Tell others about your
site.

- Get on Google News.
- Use Snip.ly.
- Interview guests.
- Write reviews.
- Create your own forum.
- Create an app.
- Create a bookmarklet or browser extension.
- Add related posts to an article.
- Make a Udemy course.
- Email out your news posts.
- Send out push notifications.
- Link to other blogs.
- Try Facebook ads.
- Get ahead with Google Ads.
- Promote with Pinterest Ads.
- Share articles on HackerNews.
- Share posts on ManageWP.
- Leave a link on Github.
- Share posts on Inbound.org.
- Find the right hosting company.
- Automatically share posts with Edgar.
- Join Triberr.

- Incorporate tweetable links.
- Update your old articles.
- Rewrite old articles.
- Proofread.
- Join Product Hunt.
- Give business cards.
- Print links.
- Make use of hashtags.
- Use stickers.
- Print out T-shirts.
- Use SliderShare.
- Create e-books.
- Make a popular post sticky.
- Sell on Marketplaces.
- Use landing pages.
- Share catchy quotes.
- Know when to publish.
- Convert articles to PDFs.
- Host free workshops.
- Advertise with Bing Ads.
- Get started with mobile ads.
- Buy ads.
- Use polls.
- Ask readers what they want to know.
- Submit your blog to all search engines.

Blogs are important to the internet. It ranges from someone's journal to informational websites, from assertive writers to helpful coaches, and from anything under the sun to lines in between, a blog has it all. Individuals and groups have the freedom to voice their thoughts and concerns and share them with millions in the world through the power of the internet. A blog, by definition and niches, is vague. There are too many definitions for it that it is hard to pin down to only one, and a lot of niches that cover various topics from as simple as parenthood to as strange as aliens. The most popular blogging niches, however, cover health and fitness, personal finance and development, food blogging, and beauty and fashion. Blogs can be written in many different styles. It can be introspective to a person's life, or it can also influence politics and business which has the power to change the world. Whatever the blog's style is, there are some universal characteristics they all share. These characteristics are what make these blogs readable and connectible to the readers. We provided you the top ten blog characteristics you should know to write well-crafted and highly engaging blog articles. Does a blog relate to the website? If so, how? Are they the same? Or are they different? Websites are used to present, but blogs are used to connect. In other words, websites are stagnant, whereas blogs are more active and engaging for you to connect to your readers. Website information posted on their pages does not require regular updates. It can stay the same for as long as website owners want. Conversely for blog posts, it requires updates like writing on your journal entries. Publishing dates and meta tags are included in blog posts, and posting new entries consistently is the key to a successful blog. Posts are Displayed with Recent Ones First Blog posts are shown differently unlike personal diaries in a notebook. For blog posts, the most recent one is always displayed on top, while the older ones are at the bottom. It is in chronologically reverse order. Your newest posts toss your old posts down the list until they do not appear on the landing page anymore. Older posts do not completely disappear though. They are only archived on the next pages. Some bloggers categorize them by year or month of publishing for easy management and organizing. Though not all, but most blog sites use a similar structure. First, there is a header with a menu to systemize the page and make a clean and neat impression to readers. The main content area follows suit. This is where blog posts appear by relevance or date of publishing. At the bottom part of blogs are terms and conditions, contact pages, and relevant links about the blog. These are all arranged neatly in a footer. There is also a sidebar which brings to light famous entries, social profiles and moves to action. Each blog has their specific niches where their posts revolve around. Posts can be of different types such as photos, videos, and written articles, among others. Most blog posts, however, are in the form of writing. Blog articles can be written as an opinion piece, current events post, or instructional guides depending on how the author of blogger wants it to be. To make the posts more engaging and visually appealing, images and videos are inserted in-between texts. On the other hand, travel and fashion blogs are usually of a different kind. Instead of focusing on words, bloggers of these blogs focus more on photos and videos with no to minimal captions. Business-related blogs also post infographics to relay information instead of instructional articles. Regardless of the style of blog content, what is important is the quality of the published content. Headlines are especially important in getting more readers. Making titles for blog posts is not an easy feat. One does not just put words together to make headlines. He/she needs to learn the art of making an appealing one. An effective headline should be able to generate clicks and drive traffic. It should also lure readers to read on or see what you have published. Blog posts should have relevant content to stimulate interest and open discussions between people. Blogs should be original and unique at the same time regardless of what types they are, the medium used, and the formats and styles. Most importantly, a blog post should deliver what it promises to its readers: engaging and relevant content related to the niche, as well as the headlines. Blogs and links are two peas in a pod. When you check decent blog websites, you can see how they all share the same characteristics in link building. Link building allows bloggers to promote their blogs and content more to the readers. Internal linking allows bloggers to lead readers to other relevant posts on their website and increase traffic along with providing a great reading experience. Whether it is done as a marketing strategy or not, it is a good way for knowledge and opinions to be shared in a systematic way. Just like a diary, blogs should also be as personalized as possible. A little flair of personal touch makes the blog more relatable and engaging. A weblog is a personal online journal that has been around for ages. The term blog originated from that word, which only heightened the importance of personal touch on a blog. As blogs evolved from private to more public issues such as politics, what remains through this day is how interpretative blog posts are. When posts require neutrality, personal touches are evident in the individual's form of writing. Each blog has the "About Me" section where authors talk about themselves and a personalized brand signature. Most engaging blogs have the comment section where readers can say their piece. The comment section is typically found at the end of every published blog content. This section aims to engage readers in a conversation and provide them an opportunity to give their feedback to the author regarding the post. When bloggers generate reaction and response from readers, it means that he/she is on the right track. With or without discussions, the main goal of a blog post is still communication. The end purpose of blogs is to convey a message that bloggers want to tell their readers. For example, promotional blogs are published to attract customers and open discussion between readers and the blogger in a move to convince them to purchase the product. If no sales are generated, at the very least, there was a move to spread the word and ultimately widen the target market. Blogging is one of the best ways to communicate with the world whether you want to share knowledge, entertain people, or provide solutions to problems. Communication, which freely expresses your opinion and response from the public, is the most important characteristic of a great blog. Blogs are not one click, and you are done. Creating blog posts, even one, means you must spend time and effort into making quality content. Investing your time and effort can help generate more traffic to your site. Aside from time and effort, other factors also influence your blog. Some of these factors include your chosen niche, audience, and style of content. But regardless of how varied your blog posts are, you must be aware of the things listed below if you want to make a good impact on your readers. 50 milliseconds are what it takes for you to make a good impression on your readers. That is why you must be careful of how you layout your blog posts. If you just put on words without visuals, it tends to be boring and you will lose the most important 50 milliseconds of your blog post's time to shine. The best layout for blogs is to break out texts from each other so they can be read easily and insert photos that are appealing in-between paragraphs. You can even make use of videos, GIFs, and other interesting visuals to make it lively. The length of the post is one of the many concerns of bloggers and soon-to-be bloggers. How long does each blog post take? Many people believe that posts should be kept short considering the short attention span of readers. Take note that there are also readers who can read lengthy posts from start to finish without losing focus. The trick to the length relies on how engaging your post is. If your posts contain valuable information and are written in a way that does not bore the readers, you can have it if you want. Do not settle for a 500-word post blog if you have more to say. Likewise, do not make a 3000-word blog if you can finish writing it in just 500 words. You should concentrate on the quality of the content above anything else. You do not have to worry about the length if you have the value your reader needs. You can never have a unique niche because whether you like it or not someone has already covered that niche before. But one thing you must do, do not ever copy-paste content from other blog sites. For you to offer original and unique content that can be considered "different" from other sites of the same niche, you must provide a different approach to the same topics that have already been covered. To approach differently, you can have an original and unique style of writing or tone of voice when presenting different ideas, or even a different point of view from other sites. As said earlier, time and effort should be invested in creating blog content. This time and effort should also be invested in research. Research is important to produce informative and quality content. Researching makes it easy to produce unique content because it gives you insights into past published articles as well as readers' opinions of the topic. It allows you to dig deeper into the topic which can lead to a more comprehensive and unique output. Without research, you may produce unreliable content which is a big no-no for a blog site. Producing unreliable content can make you lose your readers too. Hence, you have to back-up every claim you raised by evidence such as supplementing links and citations from reliable sources. Got the Courage to Start Your Blog? Once you decide to start your own blog, you need to follow these steps. First, choose the blogging platform and your blog's name. The most recommended self-hosted platform is WordPress.org. Second, you need to choose your web hosting service. Bluehost is recommended for new bloggers. They offer a free domain name once you sign up and provide you with a 30-day money-back guarantee. WordPress.org works well with Bluehost as they described the latter as "one of the best and brightest of the hosting world." Blogging is very vague when defined, but do not let it stop you. Any blogger sees that the beauty of blogging comes from how diverse it is. The characteristics we have presented are more of a guideline than rules, except for communication. Communication is the heart of blogging and everything else is set to engage and please our readers.

Chapter 10
How to Sell Ads on Your Blog

M any people make money writing blogs nowadays. If you have your blog website, you can make money by selling ads. Some of the bloggers founded their blogs because of the thought of earning huge sums of money through ads. This method of earning is legit and very convenient to do. However, most of your readers and followers hate seeing ads and become irritated when one ad pops up from somewhere. As a blogger, you need to discover the best way to make ads work without annoying your followers. Let us be honest here, writing blogs is easy but constructing a blog site that is appropriate for ad space is tricky. Do not give up though! You can still create your dream blog while earning cash from ad space if you read and follow through our tips down below. Before you proceed any further, it is important to keep in mind that making money out of your blog takes a systematic process. You cannot make money out of it as soon as you start blogging. But if you are an influencer that has an established blog already which can generate lots of traffic through your followers, you can sell space for ads and generate money this way. In creating a blog appropriate for ads, you must think about the amount of traffic, stability, and your blog's design. These requirements are important because these are what entice an advertiser to pay you for an ad on your blog. For advertisers to get interested in your blog, you must have at least 10,000 blog visitors per month. This may be hard to achieve if you are a start-up blogger, but over time and with great contents and marketing, this number is highly achievable. A professional blog design with spaces for ads is also a must because advertisers are looking for layouts which can highlight their advertisements. Moreover, the stability of a blog focuses on generating constant traffic. You need to maintain your number of blog visitors per month, and it will be best if it keeps growing in number over time. Advertisers want to rent an ad space that many people can see and read. What are the Ads You can Sell on Your Blog? You can post different types of ads on your blog. You need to know what these different types are for you to distinguish which among the different types work better for your blog, and which you must stay away from. Google AdSense (PPC). PPC or pay-per-click is one of the ways at which you as a blogger can earn from ads on your website. Google AdSense allows website owners to place targeted ads on their respective sites. When these ads are clicked on by a website visitor, it generates income to the blogger. You do not have to work on it directly since it is the advertiser who will put the ads on your blog. As the website's founder, what you need to do is to make an AdSense campaign that is relevant to what your blog is all about. If you choose random ads that are in no way connected to your blog, it will only generate negative results. For example, if you run a blog about weddings, advertise ads related to weddings such as wedding gown boutiques, flower shops and photography ads. If you blog about health-related contents, only put up ads that are related to health such as pharmaceuticals, gym and food ads. Prices on AdSense are paid dynamically and are set through an auction. Hence, it is hard to give an exact amount to how much a blogger can make from using AdSense. A lot of websites get profit using AdSense, but you must check on it first if it is the best one for you. Also, try optimizing the ads on your site to help increase revenue. Affiliate Links. Affiliate marketing involves earning a commission every time you promote other people's products by inserting an affiliate link on your posts. An affiliate link is a specific URL which has the affiliate's details. If you have a large following on your blog, it is guaranteed that your followers trust you and values your opinion. When you write contents with affiliate links, chances are they will consider your suggestion and check out the link you have posted. Every time you can insert a link into your content, do so. It is a chance to promote other products and give you revenues. Getting paid through affiliate links, however, is different from getting paid through PPC. In affiliate links, the advertiser will only pay you if a reader clicks on the link and complete a certain action such as making a purchase or registering for a subscription. To get better revenues through affiliate links, make sure that you put the links in the right parts of your blog. Make sure that you have build-up the product before inserting the link in the content so that your readers have an idea of what they are clicking into. Furthermore, do not insert misleading links nor deceive your followers by advertising poor products and services. Not only will this tarnish your reputation as a blogger, but you can also lose some of your followers. Amazon Affiliate Program. Amazon is one of the largest and most famous online marketplaces. The Amazon Affiliate Program can be considered as a blogger's pot of gold. Each product sold through an affiliate link gives you up to 10% of the advertising commission. 10% may be small for some of you, but once you get the hang of the process and many people purchase through the links you provided, you can generate a good amount of income. If you are a tech blogger, you can write reviews on different gadgets such as phones, laptops, and other devices. You can insert an Amazon affiliate link which will lead your readers to your reviewed products in Amazon. The blog comes naturally as you reviewed a product for them and provided them with a link should they choose to buy one for themselves. One tricky thing though is the geolocation of the affiliate program. Make sure that you put appropriate links based on where your readers are located. Banners, links, and widgets may also be included on your post. If you do this right, you will surely earn big bucks from the Amazon Affiliate Program. Direct Advertising. Direct Advertising allows you to reach out to advertisers so that they choose your blog for their advertising campaigns. In this type of advertising, you do not need a third party to facilitate your advertising gigs as you are placing your own advertisement on your own blog saying that the exact spot is for rented ads. This type of advertising requires your blog to have good traffic and reaches a wide range of audience for advertisers to consider renting your ad space. Sponsored Blog Posts. Sponsored blog posts mean articles written by other people that are published on your blog site. There are occasional moments though that you, as the primary blogger, must write these articles. Mostly, you will receive an article that you can publish on your blog. As the owner of the website, you may recommend some edits or request to get paid in return of writing a blog for them. Do not ever accept free sponsored blog posts except when the request comes from big-time bloggers who can help your site get more followers. When accepting sponsored blog posts, you must make sure that you accept only the things that are related to your blog's theme. As the owner of the site, you can request specific contents that you want to post and can take advantage of these articles to fill in spaces on your blog while making a profit out of it. Chitika. Chitika is an ad network suitable for bloggers with a lot of search engine traffic. It is a great substitute for AdSense. This ad network shows effective and relevant ads if your blog has not reached strong traffic yet. Chitika offers different ad types on their system, and they are easy to make and customize. Its primary domain is contextual ads. You can also find hover ads, in-text ads, and highlight ads. Chitika is a large-scale blogger's pot of gold, but even small ones can make money out of it too. BuySellAds. This is a network where bloggers can connect with potential advertisers. Biggest niche blogs also rely on BuySellAds for their advertising gigs. One downside on using this network, however, is the fact that they are very costly. BuySellAds takes 25% from every ad sale that you have. The upside is that they help with payments, ad hosting as well as bookkeeping, which makes the process of advertising transactions smooth and easy. Blogs have quality leads you can use for various ad strategies. Blogs should be able to talk about topics that generate interests among people, especially those topics that are vital in their daily living and provides them with information to solve existing problems. Quality contents mean appealing topics. If you want to achieve a strong lead, you need to produce quality contents that appeal to the public. It may sound easy, but it can be difficult to settle on one niche alone. To help minimize your choices, ask yourself what problems people have and what advice you give them to help find a solution to their problems. Choosing your blog's topics matter, therefore think about what you want to write carefully. You can take other ideas from similar blogs but do not copy them altogether. You can check it out to inspire you for more ideas or how to deal with a similar matter from a different angle. Blog posts should be published consistently and shared on different social media platforms for better exposure and increase traffic. You should also include helpful external links that will direct readers to other contents on your blog. Providing quality contents that are honest and reliable will make people trust you and your blog. Once trust has been built you can now lead your readers to paid ads for which you can earn revenues. Make sure that you only direct them to products and services that offer quality and class. Do not ever compromise your integrity for paid ads, which provides lousy products and services. There are two important factors on selling ads: your blog and your readers. Your blog should make an impact online and must remain classy so that it will not reduce the quality of your posts nor the reading experience of your followers once you add advertisements. Remember, your readers control traffic and you need to keep them interested in your contents so that advertising companies will choose you. Good luck on your blog endeavor! Did you know that you can bring in cash from the web? Making money online is now a trend because it is easy and convenient to do so... add on to that the extra cash you will earn! You can start an online business as a side- hustle for extra cash without even quitting your regular job. A lot of people are selling things online because it brings in extra revenue and has a positive result. However, just like in any businesses, you must be aware that there are different approaches you must learn and take into consideration. There are two things that you can sell online: digital and physical. When you sell online, you must decide between selling digital products or physical products. Or you can even do both if you like. Digital products are those you can buy virtually and stay virtually such as eBooks, digital music, or online courses. On the other hand, physical products involve things that you can touch and are delivered to you like toys, clothes, and actual books. In selling digital and physical products online, you must know the ins and outs of the online world. You must ensure that you are well-equipped to get in touch with your target market so that your efforts will bring positive results and profit. What are the Advantages of E-commerce? It may not feel like it, but e-commerce has been around for ages! Though we have only seen the obvious rise of e-commerce in recent years, the start of online transactions began before the 21st century even started. Despite many people favor online shopping nowadays; we still have not realized the importance and advantages of this new method of purchasing brings to our society. E-commerce allows sellers to reach audiences all around the globe, thereby increasing sales in the process. One of the benefits of e-commerce and selling your products on an online store or online marketplace is the fact that the internet does not stop. Your website is up 24 hours, 7 days a week where potential customers can browse and purchase your products anytime – even when you are sleeping. With the presence of thousands of e-commerce websites, people can buy anything they want without leaving their homes. This convenience is one of the main reasons why the e-commerce industry continues to rise. You should take this opportunity to start selling your products online as well to generate more sales. Starting up an e-commerce-based business is easier than setting up a physical store. Starting up your business website is not as costly as renting a space for your shop. Maintenance fees for an online business website are also low compared to maintaining an actual store. In addition, an online business allows you to keep track of your business faster and effortlessly. With tons of online shoppers in the world, you can cater to them all and provide them with your best products and exemplary customer service seamlessly. There is no point in why you should not open an online business when everything is in favor of you. What are the Best Online Store Solutions? You cannot sell online products without building your online store. To help build your online store, there are several online store solutions available on the web. Each online store solutions differ from what they offer, their pricing, as well as how user-friendly their platforms are. The list below highlights the best and most popular online store solutions you can use to start your online business and sell your products online: BigCommerce. Like Shopify, BigCommerce provides an excellent 24/ 7 quality support to sellers using their platform. With the extensive features this online store solution provides, it makes it extremely easy for sellers and purchasers to navigate the site when selling and buying. BigCommerce does not have transaction fees. However, most of the design themes they provide for sellers are paid. The different themes are mobile-friendly and allow you to personalize your store to help it stand out among the other stores. Recently, the platform introduced BigCommerce Plug-in for WordPress that allows you to sell your products easily in any WordPress site page. PinnacleCart. PinnacleCart is intended for business owners who prefer more control of their online store. This platform allows you to build an online shop easily and keep track of progress conveniently. What makes PinnacleCart unique from the other online store solutions is that it allows sellers to make a fully customized shop which can meet even the most bizarre and unique needs and ideas of businesses. The platform also provides an array of services designed for business growth such as live chat, customer support, store management and many more. Though it is pricey compared to other online store solutions, this platform provides top-notched features which are worth every penny you spend on it. SHOPIFY. One of the most popular e-commerce platforms is Shopify. It has more than 400,000 online stores making it one of the largest online store solutions there is. It also allows a seller to sell products at a retail site. In Shopify, you can upload as many products as you have and can create a customized list for these products. The platform also makes it easy for sellers to track leads and conversions. When it comes to designing your online shop, Shopify offers 100 themes for the design you want to use with 1400 plug-ins that improves your shop's functionality. Moreover, Shopify has a mobile app for easy access. It can also be integrated with social media apps. If you have any issues with regards to selling or technical difficulties, the 24/7 live chat support is always there to help you with your needs. WEEBLY. If you are looking for affordable, don't look any further and go directly to Weebly. It is one of the most affordable website builders that most sellers are using to build their e-commerce stores. Weebly offers uploading unlimited products that you can offer in your online store and provides you with fresh template designs and attractive layouts. Aside from being affordable, it is also known as a user-friendly platform since it is easy to navigate even for people who do not have any ideas on how to make websites. It also offers 24/7 support and can be downloaded as a mobile app as well. WooCommerce. WooCommerce is another e-commerce platform that is popular among sellers. It has hundreds of themes and plug-ins and provides sellers several great features that enable customization in the seller's online shop with the WordPress Content Management System. It is important to note that before installing WooCommerce, you must have WordPress first to proceed with the installation. 3dcart. An all-in-one store builder which is considered one of the best e-commerce platforms for Search Engine Optimization (SEO). 3dcart's design conventions are favored by Google leading to a boost in your website's search engine ranking. Though it does not provide as many plug-ins as the other online store solutions, 3dcart recompense for it with tons of built-in features that include marketing & SEO, secure hosting, -and customer support. Selling Digital and Physical Products Online: What is the Difference? Before putting up your products to sell online, you must know the difference between digital and physical products. As said earlier, digital products are those that are virtually sold and acquired. These products are things you can sell constantly without the physical distribution of goods nor manufacturing costs. Digital products can be acquired through a simple download at your customer's end. Your clients will receive the purchased digital item in a file format compatible with their device. More examples of digital products being sold online are software, website themes, digital photographs, digital artworks, and graphics. Meanwhile, physical products are those products that are tangible which customers can lay their hands on and touch. As a seller, you need to ship the actual items to your customers once they finished their purchase online. Included in this category are items from grocery, apparel, merchandise, and everything that requires real shipment and delivery of objects. Another difference between the two products is the method with which they are sold. To sell physical products, you need a traditional e-commerce store. However, to sell digital items, you only need a website where you can place and advertise your goods for clients to buy and download by themselves. Knowing the difference between digital and physical selling allows you to provide the exact services your client needs. You must think of what type of products you want to sell and choose one of the online store solutions that are designed for products you sell. After you have decided on your product/s and online store solutions, you need a marketing strategy to engage your potential consumers and make them buy your products. Marketing online shops and products allow you to advertise your store to gain more traction in selling. Since you offer your products and services alone, it is also best to advertise online in different ways. Blogging is one of the most common ways to promote a business. Once your online store is up and running, you need to start a blog. Your blogs should talk about your different products where you highlight each of their best features and what your customers can get from buying it. It is important to produce blogs that are engaging and have compelling content so that visitors who are reading your blogs will stay longer on your site. You have to take note that you have to publish fresh content on a regular basis to increase more traffic on your site as well as engage your customers by having something to look forward to from you every now and then. Inserting appropriate images on your blog posts is strongly recommended to make your posts more appealing. Videos for blogs such as testimonials and tutorials are also recommended since it connects more to your consumers than just words. Extending your connections by reaching out to influential bloggers also helps a lot and may generate a strong and avid following. E-MAIL MARKETING. Sending e-mails to your target audience is powerful in marketing. When you send an e-mail to a potential client, you generate leads and share important information about the products you are selling. You must have a subscription option on your online store so that customers can subscribe to your e-mail list. With this subscription list, you can send out e-mails to promote new products, offer discounts, and encourage them to read your blogs. You can increase your blog subscriber base using other options such as posting on forums or starting a podcast. Incorporating such ways will help increase your sales and profit. SOCIAL MEDIA MARKETING. The age of social media makes it easy for sellers to advertise their products and services. It allows the expansion of advertising to reach a global audience and establishing your products on different mediums that can best promote what you are offering. Encouraging your followers and customers to provide testimonials about your products is helpful in advertising and building trust among your clientele. Engagement on social media such as replying to comments and messages is essential in building a good reputation for your online business. People will feel that your online shop is customer centered as you consider everything they say. Connection is the best way to increase engagement and a strong customer base for your brand. Furthermore, social media platforms allow you to create poll questions, contests and some other exciting promotions that will entice your followers, and future followers, to join the different activities you set while promoting your products in the process. PPC (Pay-Per-Click) ADVERTISING. Most start-up businesses avoid PPC advertising since it can be costly at times. However, if this method is set-up appropriately, it will lead to increase revenue that can surpass whatever you have spent on this marketing strategy. PPC advertising increases website traffic to attract quality leads, thereby increasing sales and revenue from a targeted demographic. A payment gateway is a service provided by your online store solution which allows credit cards or direct payments to e-commerce retailers like you. A payment gateway verifies clients' credit card details so that payments are made accordingly. Payment gateways are not the same as merchant accounts, which holds funds prior to sending it to your bank account. The primary job of payment gateways is to approve or decline transactions. They only pass your customer's credit card information to a merchant. Once it is approved, the payment is deposited into your account. Several payment gateways, meanwhile, do not use merchant accounts such as Paypal and Stripe. These payment gateways confirm credit card information and directly transfer the money to your bank account if there is no problem with the verification process. One of the downsides of these payment gateways, however, is that they charge higher fees in every transaction you make. As your business grows, the fees may also grow. Online selling of digital and physical products is relatively easy when you know the ins and outs of the system. Setting up your online store is simple nowadays. If you properly make use of several marketing strategies to your advantage, you can generate income 24/7! If you read it until here, then you are well-equipped to start your e-commerce store. Choose the best online shop solution for your products, advertise your online store accordingly, and start building a loyal base of customers by providing engaging contents and excellent customer service. When starting a blog, the first major decision you will have to make is the kind of content to create. This article brings a long list of content types. Hopefully, you will find something that interests you. The list is divided into three major groups:

- Textual content
- Multimedia content
- Other

Textual Content
This type of content does not require video or audio material. You only need to arrange words into compelling text.

- Blog posts (long, consistent text)
- Articles such as announcements and news
- How-to instructions for readers
- Guides that share knowledge
- Top "X" lists
- Q & A
- Case studies
- Testimonials (what clients say about you)
- Interviews
- Product reviews
- Checklists
- Research—sharing your findings
- White papers for technical information
- Industry news
- Company news
- Guest posts—let other bloggers post on your site
- Personal stories

- Success stories
- Personal bios
- Comments (readers' feedback)
- FAQs section
- Glossary
- Wikis
- Versus articles
- Comparisons
- Predictions
- Inspirational messages (this is a good way to go viral)
- Content on avoiding failure
- Interesting facts
- Funny stories
- Quotes by famous people
- Literary works
- Microblog posts (short valuable content)
- Best practice experiences
- Metaphors
- Scheduled events (so your audience can meet you)
- "Why" content
- Cost sheet
- Product announcements
- Newsletters
- Promoted posts
- Recipes
- Disclaimers

Multimedia Content

Here, you mix different kinds of materials. It is a large group that includes pictures, audio, video, or a combination of them all.

- Infographics (for statistics, facts, etc.)
- Cheat sheets

- eBooks
- Screenshots
- Audio posts
- Audiobooks
- Photography (post your work)
- Podcasts
- Vlogs (e.g. travel vlogs)
- Live videos
- Micro videos (short, promotional videos)
- Presentations
- Webinars
- Polls
- Online events
- Courses
- Surveys (gather opinions and data)
- Roundups
- SlideShare's (create and post slideshows)
- Data visualization (portray data with graphs and charts)
- Data collecting (post cool research results or data)
- Diagrams
- Illustrations (tell a story with pictures)
- GIFs (best for social networks)
- Demonstration (e.g. how something works)
- Transparency
- Posters
- Memes (graphic content for entertainment or comedy)
- Cartoons and comics (create something funny and interesting)
- Competitions (contests for your audience)
- Online magazine
- Fun quizzes
- Music videos

- Public service announcements (PSA)
- Maps—show historical places
- Forums for people to discuss various issues
- Fan page for your favorite celebrity
- Media mentions—show what the media says about your business
- Giveaways- people cannot say no to free stuff
- Feature pages
- Daily shows—talk to your audience regularly about anything

Other

- Plugins that could be useful for readers
- Templates
- Free tools
- Browser extensions—integrate your content into browsers
- QR codes
- Free resources for readers to download
- Chat rooms for visitors to share information
- Mobile apps
- Countdowns to significant events
- Social network buttons
- Calculators
- Converters for different units
- User generated content (allow visitors to post)
- Collaborations with fellow bloggers
- Email campaign
- Landing pages
- Promo-sites (promoting services or products)
- Income reports
- Best awards
- Online games (simple browser games to attract visitors)
- Offline magazines—scan and post printed magazines

- Swag—send branded little gifts to your audience
- Ads

Content does not have to be long articles. Use different forms of content to attract a wide audience. Selling your services online, just like selling products, requires you to have an online store or a virtual business card. Even with a website, you will still have to get the word out. That is how potential customers will know of your existence. This post is a comprehensive guide to selling your services online. Other than building a website and having a "contact me" page, there is a lot more information that you need to include. Potential customers need to know that they can trust you. Here is how you can prove your credibility: Testimonials appeal to clients emotionally. Most people trust the experiences of other customers and use them to make a purchase decision. Create video testimonials and post them on the website. In addition to testimonials, make it possible for clients to leave reviews. They build credibility and act as constructive feedback. Use them to see what you can improve about your business. Optimize the site for search engines for more traffic. SEO boosts organic traffic and grows your customer base. SEO is not a one-time thing. You must keep improving the website. A blog engages your customers. You can tell the brand's story and give detailed information about your services. Explain how the experience will be like and what benefits the client will enjoy. Make the content intriguing, useful and relevant. Remember to use relevant keywords too. SEO techniques can bring people to your website. But to get to more potential customers, you need to try other ways. Build a social media presence and make sure you use it. Social media platforms attract tons of active users daily. Some networks are better than others when it comes to reaching the target audience. Research thoroughly to know where the target audience is. If you want more opportunities, networking must be at the top of your list. Connect with people who will take you further than you would go alone. Contact influential bloggers and ask them to promote your website. In exchange, promote them on your blog. Attend networking events and have a conversation with industry leaders. There are many freelancing platforms and they allow you to sell your services. Many people use them daily. Find one or more and create a profile. Include your experience, qualifications, and skills. Make sure clients know the value you will add to their business. A good reputation will strengthen your relationship with clients. They may also refer you to other clients. Deliver on promises. Offer exactly what a customer need. Resolve customer complaints. Respond to negative feedback and give solutions. Be consistent. Retain Old Customers and Build a Customer Network - Follow up with clients to see if they are satisfied and let them know that you care. This inspires loyalty. Thank them for trusting you with their project too.

Chapter 11
Tips That Guarantee More Blog Subscribers

It is easy to forget about your subscribers as a blogger. If you want to reach a larger audience and become successful, you need to focus more on your subscribers. What is the use of having high-quality content if no one reads it? Always think about how to attract visitors and convert them into subscribers. Not every blog post will be a success. Some will get more views than others. When an article gets a lot of views, it shows you that readers find it useful and interesting. Use it to earn more subscribers. First, optimize them for subscription. In all your popular blog posts, include an irresistible CTA (call-to-action). Encourage readers to subscribe for more high-quality articles. You can place the CTA at the end of the post or make it a slide-in or pop-up. A Subscribe Widget is a widely used approach by bloggers. At the end of every article, include a subscribe box. If readers like the post, they will be compelled to subscribe for more. It could be something like, "subscribe to receive exclusive tips in your inbox." The landing page should be appealing, with relevant information and a compelling CTA. Guide the visitors to receive the latest content or enroll in a course. Place a by-line link in the section where you show the author's name. Make it visible by placing it below the blog post headline. Make use of sidebar white space, especially in lengthy posts, by including a sticky widget. This captures the attention of the reader. The widget stays stuck in the sidebar even as people scroll. Hello-bars are captivating—no wonder they are becoming more popular. A hello-bar is a useful toolbar at the top of the website. It engages visitors as soon as they open your blog. Use it to amplify subscriptions. This pop-up message captures a visitor before they exit. It persuades the reader to stay longer and probably subscribe. Note that pop-ups can be irritating. So, make it irresistible. The welcome gate is shown to first-time visitors. It is usually an interesting CTA, convincing them to subscribe. Leverage CTA: make your CTAs count. The reader should want to give you their email address. If you have a primary and secondary CTA, they should complement and not compete with one another. Automated CTA: a smart CTA will show different messages depending on the visitor. Approaching potential subscribers properly: contact potential subscribers directly. Be confident and direct, but not disrespectful. Mobile optimization: mobile devices are used way more than desktops. Give the users a seamless experience. A/B split testing: use and compare a few CTAs to see which one works best. Expand to social media: share your blog on social networks to get to more people. Subscription visibility: make your subscription buttons visible.

Only ask for what you need: long forms are annoying and may turn away subscribers. Cross-promotional agreements: talk to fellow top bloggers and make a cross-promotional agreement. If you are a digital marketing newbie, you may not know what evergreen content means. It is popular in the content marketing community and is a major factor if you want to achieve content strategy success. So, here is everything you need to know about evergreen content. Evergreen content remains relevant to your readers. It offers value, years after you have published it. It stays fresh over time—hence the name "evergreen". Knowing what is not considered evergreen is also important. Take news articles, for instance. They cannot be considered evergreen because they talk about current events and come with an end date. Readers may visit them from time to time to get information about an earlier event. However, you cannot expect regular traffic. The same applies to statistical reports. Over time, the numbers will change. Again, someone may check the content out for comparative reasons, but you won't get regular traffic.

Current trends content is not evergreen too. Summer tips and fashion advice will not be relevant come winter, for example. This goes for content designed for specific seasons such as Thanksgiving and Christmas as well. So now you know what evergreen content is and what it is not. But do you know what makes it important and valuable? Check out its benefits. Evergreen content is more valued by search engines than old content. They crawl web pages for content analysis. If you have valuable content that is optimized for specific keywords, it will start ranking higher in search results. With a higher SEO ranking, your blog will start getting more traffic. Since the content remains valuable over time, the traffic will be consistent. Additionally, relevant content has a high chance of being shared on social networks. This means even more traffic. With more traffic, you have a higher chance of generating leads. Consequently, your opportunities and sales will increase. Make sure your evergreen articles have compelling CTAs. Your blog probably contains evergreen content already. If not, you need to start creating it as soon as possible. Here are a few types to help you get started. Lists: this kind of content is easy to digest and follow. It is simply a list of relevant and valuable information about a topic. Top tips: offer your readers the top tips to help them achieve certain goals. How-to tutorials: guides and tutorials make perfect evergreen content. Create them specifically for beginners. Encyclopedia entries: unchanging truths and facts are also considered evergreen content. Evergreen Content Examples - How to create a website for beginners. The beginner's ultimate guide to SEO. Top travel destination articles (for example, the world's top romantic destinations). Glossary (for example, content marketing glossary). To come up with evergreen content, think of something that will offer value to readers for a long time. Be sure to revisit the content and update it as needed. Blogs began as online journals where people shared their lives. But today, the goals are more professional. Most people now blog to promote their business or brand. This post highlights common reasons for blogging and the benefits. People love to share what they are passionate about. If you love fishing, you will want to tell the whole world about it. This goes for other things such as marketing, photography, etc. Blogging about what you love helps you connect with others who share your passion, all around the globe. A blog gives you a platform to teach others. As you do so, you will also be learning more about the subject. Educating through a blog can open a stream of income for you. Blogs for business owners increase exposure. Regular blog content earns you visibility in Google search results. And if you create content for other websites, you will expose your business to a new audience. Sharing what you know via a blog makes people view you as an authority. If you choose a specific niche, you may start getting invited to speak at events, podcasts and interviews. The more you attend, the more people know you. Eventually, you may get a book publishing contract. As highlighted above, regular blog content will make you rank in search engines. With target commercial keywords, you can attract customers. Social media audiences seem to prefer blog posts over sales pages or ads. Share your articles on social networks and allow your readers to do the same. Manage online identity: Someone can know what your business is all about when they search for it online. A blog helps you control how your business is defined. Learn new things: blogging allows you to impart knowledge. But more importantly, it helps you learn. You must research to teach others. You will also gain valuable online marketing knowledge. Improve writing skills: maintaining a blog involves creating a lot of written content. Even video bloggers and podcasters must write descriptions and engage with subscribers in the comment section. Proficiency in a new language: most people do not get to blog in their mother tongue. Writing in another language makes you more proficient. Technical Knowledge: you may not become a web design expert, but you will acquire a little tech knowledge along the way. Connect with new friends: you will develop a fanbase and probably build long-lasting relationships. Become an expert: as you continue to gain recognition in your niche, people will consider you an expert. Get invited: experts are always getting asked to speak at events. Become an author: if people like what you write, getting someone to publish your books will be easy. Job offers - other businesses will want you to create compelling content for them. A new business: your blog can become a real business if you take it seriously. Sell more products: target your ideal customer with your content and you will boost sales. Immediate feedback: readers post what they think in the comment section. More blogs: when the first blog starts paying off, you can build another one. Freedom: bloggers can work from anywhere and whenever they want.

Chapter 12

Marketing on Instagram

M edia outlets are always talking about Instagram. What is it? Well, it is not new, and it is becoming increasingly popular by the day. Instagram is a social network where people can share videos and photos using their smartphones. Just like Twitter and Facebook, you will have a newsfeed and a profile once you create Instagram. When you share a video or photo, it appears on your profile and your followers can see it on their feed. In the same way, you will see videos and photos from people you follow. Users can interact on Instagram, as is the case with other social platforms. You can follow people and get followed, private messages, like, tag and comment. If you see a photo you like, you can save it too. It is a free app that you can download for free on your iPad, iPhone, and Android devices. You can also access Instagram using your computer via the web. However, you will not be able to share existing content or upload new content. That can only be done via the mobile app. To use Instagram, you must create an account first—it is free. Sign up either through email or your Facebook account. You will need a password and username. When you first sign up, you will be prompted to follow your Facebook friends on Instagram. Skip through or follow them if you like. You may want to customize your Instagram profile first. Add a photo, name, website link and a short bio. You will need to follow people and get followers to make the experience interesting. And people will be skeptical if you do not have anything to show who you are. The main purpose of Instagram is to share photos and videos. Everyone wants to see and share the most appealing posts. Your user profile shows how many people you follow and how many follows you. If you want to follow someone, tap the follow button. If their profile is private, you will have to wait until they approve. To interact with people, like their photos by double-tapping or add a comment below the post. For follow suggestions, touch the search tab and you will see recommended users just for you. Instagram allows you to edit your photos before posting using several filters. You can take a video or photo via the app or upload from your gallery. You have 50 filters to choose from and other photo editing options. Once you are satisfied with your edits, you can move to the next tab and write a caption, post to other socials, tag a location and tag a user. Finally, publish the photo so your followers can see and interact with the post. Instagram Stories feature is at the top of the feed (the circles you see with other users' names). Tap the circles to view a story. You have probably considered Instagram at some point for your business. Or maybe you have not given it much thought. It is a popular social media platform and it is becoming better by the day. Its features make amazing marketing tools especially for small businesses. So, if you are a small business owner, here are seven reasons why you should check out Instagram. The best way to tell a story is through a video or a picture. When Instagram first started, it was marketed as a fun and beautiful way of sharing life with loved ones through pictures. That has not changed much but there have been a lot of changes. One of the things that make Instagram awesome is the fact that you can create content without even leaving the app. It is easy to use and cost-effective, making it perfect for those on a budget. The story format is here to stay. Mark Zuckerberg says that users absolutely love it and most of them say they follow businesses' Instagram stories. So, if you are looking to interact with your audience, Instagram Stories will do. Instagram is not just about sharing videos and photos. The features are set up in a way that encourages engagement. And that is what Instagram is all about. It is not enough to get people to see your content. Your audience should swipe to view more photos, comment, join in conversations, answer story polls, etc. When they do this, Instagram will know that they love your content. And they will continue to see more of your posts. Building a relationship with your customers is important. That is why you need a platform like Instagram where actual interaction happens and is encouraged. In today's world, people love binging on something. Serial content is preferred. You can leverage this in two ways: Story Highlights: convert your stories to Story Highlights. Your users will be able to watch them in series or under categories. They will be automatically taken to the next one once they are done watching the first. Instagram TV: you can create content in episodes for your viewers to keep coming back for more. You can also answer customer questions using Story Question Stickers. Most people hold their phones vertically and so a lot of content is vertical. Instagram lets you share whatever content you have in your phone spontaneously. Your audience is already using the format. The location feature on Instagram is especially useful for business owners. Tag your content to give it a higher chance of being seen by the right people. Make use of the Location Sticker on Instagram Stories. If you can, use specific locations. Getting engagement on Facebook is not easy. On Instagram, going straight to the DMs is acceptable and even expected. This allows for meaningful conversations with your followers and you get feedback too. You can then make content that suits them even better. If you want one-on-one conversations with your customers, you need to join Instagram. Many people are focused on advertising through Google, LinkedIn, Facebook, and several other sites. But they often ignore Instagram. Instagram has fewer users compared to Facebook and they are also much younger. But its influence can make a huge difference. For many advertisers, Instagram ads have turned out to be more successful than they anticipated. There are different ad formats available that allow you to display visual stories. Currently, active Instagram users are estimated at 800 million. When you think about how big of a platform Instagram is, you may wonder how your little business will stand out. And that is the point of Instagram advertising. This chapter will teach you all there is to learn about Instagram advertising. Instagram Advertising is an advertising method in which you pay to have your content sponsored and posted on Instagram to reach the relevant audience. Advertising is done for many reasons. In this case, it is done to generate new leads, increase website traffic, make your brand known and convert leads. On Instagram, visuals are everything, so you will not find text ads. You will need a video or images. Going by March 2017 statistics, Instagram advertising works. 75% of Instagram users said they were inspired to take an action by a post. Should You Try Instagram Advertising for Your Business? Unfortunately, Instagram is not the best idea if you are targeting an older audience. Over half of Instagrammers are 18 to 29 years old. Only about 15% are aged 50 years and above. More users (32%) also live in the urban areas and suburbs (28%). 18% live in the country. More women than men use Instagram, but the gender gap is getting smaller. It is likely that more adults will migrate to Instagram with time. Instagram advertising allows you to target specific behaviors, interests, locations, age ranges, gender, etc. How Much Will It Cost You to Advertise on Instagram? You cannot get a straightforward answer to this question. There are different factors that determine the cost and the platform does not reveal the factors. They use CPM (cost per impressions) and CPC (cost per click). Instagram uses their ad auction to determine prices. According to Ad Espresso, the CPC ranges from $.0.70 to $0.80. Know that this number greatly varies depending on the day of the week, time of day, competition, etc. You can end up paying a lot depending on the ad engagement. But Instagram allows you to control your budget. It may all seem complicated, but you will soon master it advertising on Instagram. If you have been using Facebook ads, this will be easy. The following steps will help you create ads using Facebook Ad Manager. Log in to Facebook and go to https://www.facebook.com/ads/manager/. You will use the Facebook Ads UI for Instagram. What is the goal of your campaign? The goal names are self-explanatory, so you will not struggle. Your goal could be increasing traffic, brand awareness, etc. For Instagram advertising, these are the only goals you can work with: Conversions (on your app or website), Video views, Engagement, App installs, Traffic (for your app or website), Reach, Brand awareness. Some of these goals will require additional steps. Look. Brand awareness: this one is simple. It will ensure that the right people see your ad. Reach: if you want more people to see your ads, select your account. Traffic: all you must do here is choose between an app and a website then input the URL. Engagement: page engagement is not yet available on Instagram so you will be paying for post engagement. App installs: choose the app store app while setting up. Video views: no additional steps. Lead generation: you will have to design a lead form. Conversions: configure an app event or Facebook pixel. Configure your target audience based on the following: Location, Age, Gender, Languages, Demographics, Interests, Behaviors, Connections. Placement Selection - If you skip this step, the ads will be shown on Facebook and Instagram. For Instagram only, go to "Edit Placements" then choose where you want your ads to appear. If you do not know where to set the budget, resort to trial and error. You can always stop or pause the campaign. Both lifetime and daily budgets have their pros and cons. Creating the Ad is where you pick an ad format. There are six Instagram ad formats—two for stories and four for the feed. Image Feed Ads is the most standard one and you have probably seen it while scrolling your Instagram feed. They are single image ads and appear natively as your audience scrolls through their feed. Image Story Ads are just like image feed ads; except they appear natively in stories. Instagram will support most video files, but they have specific recommendations. Stories usually contain videos, so users already expect them. The ad will not feel forced. Instead of one image, you can show several scrollable images. If your brand is very visual (food, furniture, etc.), this is perfect. Canvas Story Ads is a new addition. The ads offer a 360 VR experience. It only works for mobile devices. Best Instagram Advertising Practices - Give personality to every ad: make it intriguing, emotional, or goofy. The post needs to feel humanized. Contextual relevance: do not use your LinkedIn ads for Instagram. Consider the atmosphere and context. Use hashtags: do not just stick to generic hashtags. Research to see what your audience is likely to search for. And do not overdo it. Contest: giveaways and contests will help you achieve your goals faster. People love participating in competitions. And who does not like free stuff? Optimal hours: if you know your audience you will know when they are likely to be online. If not, go the trial and error way.

Chapter 13
Instagram Stats

If you plan to incorporate Instagram into your marketing strategy, there are important facts that you need to be aware of. Check them out. In 2018, Instagram was the second most downloaded app in the App Store. Instagram is among the top 10 most popular queries on Google. Instagram video views and like counts are now hidden in seven countries (and six more by July). Instagram has one billion users every month. Instagram Stories attract 500 million users every day. The Stories feature is one of the reasons why Instagram is so popular. 89% of Instagram users are outside the United States. By the end of 2020, Instagram is expected to have 112.5 million American users. In Canada, Instagram is growing faster than any other social media platform. Brunei has the highest Instagram percentage reach (60%). 37% of adults in America use Instagram. It is more popular among younger users. Most teens in the U.S prefer Instagram to other traditional social media platforms. The gender gap on Instagram has reduced. It is now 48% male and 52% female. 63% of users log in to Instagram at least one time in a day. 42% log in several times. The average amount of time spent on Instagram is 28 minutes in a day. 200 million users check out at least one Instagram business profile in a day. 62% of Instagram users admit that they develop interest in a product or brand after stumbling upon it in the Stories. 11% of social media users in the U.S shop on Instagram. Every month, 130 million users on Instagram tap on shopping posts. Over half of Instagrammers use Explore each month. Red apple emojis were posted more than green ones for back to school. In Instagram Stories, the most popular sticker is the heart love Giphy. In the US, 14% of adults use Instagram as their news source. The potential advertising reach for Instagram is 849.3 million users. Advertisers on Instagram can reach 52.9 million youths (13 to 17 years). For every post, Instagram influencers are paid from $100 to $2,085 by brands. Marketers in the U.S now use 69% of the budget allocated to influencing on Instagram. Marketers in the U.S use 31% of their Instagram ad money on Stories. In 2020, Instagram is expected to earn ad revenue worth $12.32 billion. 73% of teens in the U.S agree that the best way to reach them about promotions or products is through Instagram. In 2020, 75.3% of businesses in the U.S will use Instagram. Average number of Stories posted by brands is 2.5 per week. Businesses Stories make up a third of the most viewed Instagram Stories. 60% of businesses use an interactive element in their Instagram Stories each month. Business Stories boast of an 85% completion rate. 10.7% of all social referral shares are from Instagram to ecommerce sites. Stories stickers improve video performance about 83% of the time. The most popular type of video content on Instagram is how-to tutorials.

Chapter 14
TikTok Marketing

Many people may not know what TikTok is, yet, but you may want to incorporate it into your social media marketing strategy. Even though you have not used TikTok before, you have most likely heard about it. Videos with the TikTok logo are all over other social media platforms. Currently, TikTok has roughly 800 million active users and in January 2020, it was reported to be the most downloaded app. It is now bigger than Pinterest and Twitter. It is very possible that TikTok is here to stay. It sounds like a goldmine for marketers, doesn't it? You need to be incredibly careful, however. People go on TikTok for entertainment and you must be wise while taking your business there. This guide will teach you everything you need to know. What Is TikTok? It is a social media app for smartphones and is mostly about video content. TikTok users (otherwise known as TikTokers), take short videos, then post them on the platform after editing. They use hashtags to identify with popular categories. Much of the content posted is generally comedic. Popular genres include cooking how-to's, cringe videos, lip-syncing, and short skits. Challenges are an extremely popular phenomena on the platform. 41% of the total number of TikTokers are aged 16 to 24 years. This is the only information that the social network has released. But you can safely assume that 24- to 30-year-olds also make up a big percentage of the users.

Here are other known statistics: iPhone/Android usage: 52%/47% split. TikTok is available in 75 languages in 150 markets. 44% of TikTokers are female while 56% are male. With these statistics in mind,

TikTok would be great for your marketing strategy if your audience is young. You can either create original content or collaborate with influencers. TikTok has huge influencers, some of them with millions of subscribers. The influencers have already created a relationship with their audience, and they can easily convince them to try your products. You basically pay them to promote the products or use them on camera. Anytime you are looking for influencers, remember that relevance is better than reach. Creating your own content requires resources, creativity, and a lot of time. And you need viral content too. To make your content popular, you must hop on trends. See what hashtags trending are. Use them to create your version. Remember to wisely incorporate something about your business. Another easier way would be offering tricks, tips, how-to's or inside secrets relevant to your industry. If organic engagement seems too complicated, you can always use the TikTok advertising platform. According to TikTok, formats include but are not limited to square, vertical or horizontal images and videos. They have ad creation tool sets—Video Creation Kit and Automated Creative Optimization— to help you crate ads. The ads can appear in story, post-roll, detail page or in-feed. You also have the option to target a specific audience.

Chapter 15
TikTok Algorithm

TikTok have managed to keep their algorithm, especially for the For You page, a secret. Platforms like Instagram have been very transparent about their feed rankings. The same cannot be said of TikTok. They have not verified any details about how their algorithm works. However, the platform has been around for a while now. From observing personal first-hand experiences, you can get some valuable information about how the algorithm chooses what to show on the For You page of a specific user. Here are 5 key insights about the algorithm. Each Video's Performance Determines Its Exposure - If you have been using TikTok, you will notice that people with barely any followers get millions of views. The TikTok algorithm seems to focus more on an individual video's interactions and less on the profile. When you publish a video, it will be shown to few users on their For You page, between popular videos. Just scroll your For You page and you will notice a video with hardly any likes. So, if this video is well-received, TikTok will show it to more users. The TikTok Algorithm Considers Multiple Indicators Some of the indicators that are considered include likes, comments, shares, video completions and re-watches. For this reason, genuinely informative or entertaining videos have a high chance of doing well. Geo-Location Determines Initial Exposure - TikTok videos are first shown to people in that geo-location. This is an observation. The location greatly influences the recommended videos on your For You page. Small businesses can benefit from increased local brand awareness. And if your video is well received in your geo-location, it may be shown internationally. Tending Sounds and

Hashtags Help - If you want to increase your content's discoverability, you need to put more thought into Sounds and hashtags. Videos with trending hashtags in their caption have a high chance of being shown in Discovery pages. They may even be included in more For You pages. Now, it is not clear which hashtags will have the biggest impact. But it is assumed that #foryoupage, #foryou and #fyp increase the likelihood of videos making it to more For You pages. Other than using high traffic hashtags, you may want to include relevant hashtags as well, depending on your niche. The TikTok algorithm will understand your content better and show it to people who are interested. In the same way, trending Sounds could boost your video's visibility.

Users on TikTok choose a sound to see all the related videos. And, obviously, trending Sounds will be prioritized. Even Older Videos Can Go Viral All of a Sudden Videos on TikTok do not have a short shelf life, as is the case on networks like Instagram. All your videos are being monitored constantly—and this includes the older ones. If your video starts getting more engagement, it may go viral. It does not matter when you posted it. This usually happens when the hashtags or Sounds you used start spiking in popularity.

Chapter 16

The Complete Guide to YouTube Marketing

YouTube marketing is a great idea but there are over 50 million YouTube content creators. One way to be successful is to make sure that your content stands out.

Another way is to reach and engage your target audience. Most YouTube viewers do not like ads, so you must be creative about creating brand awareness and entertaining them at the same time. Create Your Business YouTube Channel - First, you will need a Brand Account on Google. The regular Google account only allows one person to log in. With a Brand Account, several Google accounts can sign in at the same time, if they are authorized. When you open a business YouTube account, you will be able to access the Analytics tab and see your channel stats. You can check your interaction rate, revenue generated, average watch time and view counts. The Analytics tab displays your subscriber demographics too which is valuable data. With this information, you will no longer have to rely on assumptions. Most of the information you will need is already on the competitors' channels. Check the channels and see the least and most viewed videos. The videos will let you know what the audience likes and what they are not interested in. Do not forget to read the comments as well and the video descriptions for keywords. Borrow Ideas from Your Favorite Channel - Why do you love your favorite YouTube channels so much? What grabs your attention every time? Studying your favorite YouTuber reveals the practices and techniques they use to boost engagement. Optimize Videos for SEO - YouTube SEO is especially important. Here are some helpful tips: Choose a catchy title and include the right keywords. Make your thumbnail interesting. Make the video description compelling. Add hashtags to the description. Add watermarks, bumper ads, and cards. Ask your viewers to subscribe. Schedule and Upload Your Videos - Be consistent and professional while sharing videos. Let your viewers know when you will be uploading new videos and make sure you do it at that time to earn their trust. Pick a specific day of the week. Optimize the Channel - A consistent experience on your channel will attract more viewers and convert them into subscribers. So, make sure you: Complete your profile. Organize your videos. Translate videos into other languages. There are different ad formats on YouTube. Whichever one you choose, ensure that you create catchy ads. Keep it short and sweet. Viewers trust their favorite influencers. The right influencer can quickly boost your brand. Do not control the partnership. Let the influencer do their thing naturally. Always keep an eye on YouTube Analytics. See how your numbers are changing. Another thing: read your comments! How to Create Great YouTube Videos - Follow the video specifications. Invest in good equipment. Capture attention early. Remember your mobile users. Upload longer videos. Add live-streaming events. Include end screens. The YouTube algorithm often decides what viewers will watch. Over 80% of viewers will watch what YouTube recommends. If you are trying to build your brand or increase your number of views, then the YouTube algorithm is important. YouTube is not usually transparent with advertisers or creators about how everything works. So, this article will focus on the history of its priorities. In 2005, the first ever YouTube video was uploaded. Today, 500 hours of video are uploaded every minute. How does YouTube recommend videos to its 2 billion users? 2005 to 2012: View Count The videos that got more clicks are the one that got rewarded. 2012: Watch Time Priority was given to videos that held users' attention for long. 2016: Machine Learning - The details here were not revealed. But it was based on the perceived satisfaction of viewers. 2016 to 2020: Brand Safety, Demonetization, Borderline Content - According to YouTube, they are trying to strike a balance between freedom of speech and curbing the spread of dangerous information. How the Algorithm Works in 2020 - YouTube says that their algorithm tailors the videos to suit each viewer's interests. The algorithm has two goals: To recommend the ideal video for every viewer. To ensure that viewers continue watching. It impacts the recommendation streams and search results. How It Influences Search Results

Two people may search for the exact same thing and get quite different results. These results depend on: The engagement on your videos (watch time, comments, likes). The metadata of your videos (keywords, description, title) and how they match a user's question. How It Influences Recommended Videos. The process is twofold. First, videos are ranked based on their performance analytics data. Secondly, the videos are recommended based on a viewer's watch history. How Does YouTube Determine the Algorithm? As already mentioned, the details are barely known. But YouTube has highlighted factors that influence the process: Whether people click to watch a video (the title and thumbnail are key here). Retention or watch time (for how long people watch the video). The rate of growth or velocity, that is, the rate at which the popularity of a video snowballs. The age of a video (newer videos may be given more attention to see whether they will snowball). The frequency at which a channel upload videos. Session time (how long people continue to stay on a platform after they are done watching the video). When a video is matched to a viewer, the next thing is personalization. What topics and channels do they watch? What do they have a history of engaging with? For how long do they watch? What don't they like? Improving Your Organic Search: 7 Tips - Optimize the description text of your video. Note what works and keep using it. Publish regularly. Know the perfect time to drop a new video. Make the entire video engaging. Do not forget to engage with your viewers. Convert viewers into subscribers.

Chapter 17
Pinterest for Business

Pinterest has now gone public. If you have not incorporated it into your social media marketing strategy, now would be a good time to do that. Pinterest is more than just a platform for creating dream boards. Why Should You Use Pinterest for Your Business? In the U.S, it is ranked as the 4th most popular social network. Pinterest is popular globally as well. The number of active users has grown tremendously. Visual search is becoming a common phenomenon. Women—the primary decision makers in homes—use Pinterest more than men. People use the platform to shop. Pins increase brand exposure. People use Pinterest for inspiration. Setting Up Your Pinterest Business Account - Visit pinterest.com/business/create. Enter a password and your email address. Click Create Account. Choose your location and language then add a business name. Connect your Etsy, YouTube, and/ or Instagram accounts. If you plan on running ads, inform Pinterest. Edit your business profile. Claim your website by clicking Claim (left-hand menu). Create a Board. Create a Pin. Pick a cover photo. Have the Pinterest tag somewhere on your website. Create interesting content on Pinterest, visuals are everything. Have high-quality images (and remember your mobile audience) and write a descriptive copy. Also include a great headline and your logo. According to Pinterest, you should pin something at least once a day. You will have much more success than you would if you created a board and filled it up all at once. Regular pinning makes it easier to reach more people. The best way to do this would be by using a scheduling tool like Hootsuite. Being a better planner is important here. Most Pinterest users love to plan of time. If you have seasonal content you would like to share, do it about 40 days in advance. Pick relevant holidays on Pinterest and create content around them. Connect with Pinners Using Boards - Create DIYs, tutorials or fill a board with photos of people using your product. Maybe have a board where people can share related content. Do not forget that Pinterest is a search engine and SEO still matters there. Use relevant keywords in your descriptions, pin names, board, and company. Be sure to also use hashtags. Another thing you can do to help with SEO is to pin your website content. Your strategy should focus on compelling users to make a purchase. The content you create must walk them from awareness to action. On Pinterest, you can target your ads around age, location, interests, keywords, etc. There is also the option of Actalike audiences. Pinterest will find people who are like your customers. Pinners love to shop. You should aim at making the process easy for them. Make use of the Shop tab and Shop the Look pins.

Chapter 18

LinkedIn for Business for Marketers

L inkedIn is used by over 30 million companies for business. It is more than just a social network that people use to hire top talent. Businesses are using it to sell, connect and network. So, how can you incorporate LinkedIn into your social media marketing strategy? First, you need a LinkedIn business account. Create Your LinkedIn Page - Go to the LinkedIn Marketing Solutions site and click on their LinkedIn Pages section. Click on Create Your Page. Choose your business category. Fill in your business details. Add a tagline and upload your logo. Click on Create Page. Add more details for visitors to know what your business is all about. This will also boost your ranking in LinkedIn and Google search results.

Add:

- Company description
- Location
- Hashtags
- Custom button
- Cover photo
- Multiple languages

Share the Page

Inform people that you have a LinkedIn page. Let your employees know so they can add it as their place of work. Do not forget to inform your customers too. If you have social media icons, in your newsletter or website, add one for LinkedIn as well. Feel free to add Follow and Share buttons with plugins for LinkedIn. Create a Marketing Strategy for LinkedIn - Once your company page is up and running, focus on creating a solid LinkedIn strategy. Establish the goals you want to achieve with the platform and whether you will have ads. See how your competitors are using LinkedIn too. LinkedIn is used by over 30 million companies for business. It is more than just a social network that people use to hire top talent. Businesses are using it to sell, connect and network. So, how can you incorporate LinkedIn into your social media marketing strategy? First, you need a LinkedIn business account.

Create Your LinkedIn Page

- Go to the LinkedIn Marketing Solutions site and click on their LinkedIn Pages section.
- Click on Create Your Page.
- Choose your business category.
- Fill in your business details.
- Add a tagline and upload your logo.
- Click on Create Page.

Complete the Page

Add more details for visitors to know what your business is all about. This will also boost your ranking in LinkedIn and Google search results.

Add:

- Company description
- Location
- Hashtags
- Custom button
- Cover photo
- Multiple languages

Inform people that you have a LinkedIn page. Let your employees know so they can add it as their place of work. Do not forget to inform your customers. If you have social media icons, in your newsletter or website, add one for LinkedIn as well. Feel free to add Follow and Share buttons with plugins for LinkedIn. Once your company page is up and running, focus on creating a solid LinkedIn strategy. Establish the goals you want to achieve with the platform and whether you will have ads. See how your competitors are using LinkedIn too. Come up with a posting schedule so that you will have enough time to plan content in advance.

Marketing Tips for LinkedIn

Include Rich Media in Your Posts

For all social media platforms, visual content performs better. If your posts have images, they are 98% more likely to get comments. Custom images receive more engagement compared to stock photos. Videos on LinkedIn get 5 times more engagement than any other content. Optimize Your Posts - Here are the factors that influence how posts are ranked by the LinkedIn algorithm: Engagement probability. Interest relevance. Personal connection. The algorithm shows users content that is likely to interest them from pages they relate to. So, make sure that your content is relevant and captivating. Brands that post at least once a month attract more followers than businesses that do not. Those that post once a day see even more engagement. Know the times of day to post. Live broadcasts are far more engaging on LinkedIn even more than video posts. Live videos may be for webinars, interviews, fireside chats, etc. You can even host a virtual event. You could use a Showcase Page to engage a target audience or show off a unique initiative. It is a way for users to follow you without necessarily following your page. LinkedIn analytics show your numbers. Use the numbers to know what to change and what is working. LinkedIn allows you to target people organically in your posts. For even better results, you can include ads in your strategy. Come up with a posting schedule so that you will have enough time to plan content in advance. On all social media platforms, visual content performs better. If your posts have images, they are 98% more likely to get comments. Custom images receive more engagement compared to stock photos. Videos on LinkedIn get 5 times more engagement than any other content. Here are the factors that influence how posts are ranked by the LinkedIn algorithm: Engagement probability. Interest relevance. Personal connections. The algorithm shows users content that is likely to interest them from pages they relate to. So, make sure that your content is relevant and captivating. Brands that post at least once a month attract more followers than businesses that do not. Those that post once a day see even more engagement. Know the times of day to post. Some businesses have already incorporated LinkedIn into their marketing strategy. Others are wondering if they should do the same. Regardless of your current situation, the following statistics will be useful in helping you plan your next move. There are 675 million monthly users on LinkedIn. Compared to 2018, this is a 14% increase. Twitter has 330 million, Instagram 1 billion and Facebook 2.5 billion. LinkedIn has 43% female users and 57% male users. 29% of men in America are on LinkedIn. Only 24% of the women in America are on the platform. 27% of Americans are LinkedIn users. The number has increased by 2% from 2018. LinkedIn is now the fifth most popular social network in America. 51% of college-educated Americans use LinkedIn. For this group, it is more popular than Pinterest and Instagram. 70% of those who use LinkedIn are not in the U.S. America remains LinkedIn's largest market, but the rest of the world is catching up. 61% of users on LinkedIn are 25 – 34 years old. The professional network is not extremely popular with the oldest and youngest age categories. 57% of users access LinkedIn on mobile. This means that you should always optimize content for mobile. LinkedIn sees 15 times more impressions for content than for job postings. Content marketers can greatly benefit from the platform. Engagement on LinkedIn has increased 50%. The algorithm has been updated to prioritize personal connections, ensuring that users see relevant content. LinkedIn users are 60% less likely to engage with a connection than they are with a coworker. Engaging here refers to messaging, sharing, commenting, and liking. 30% of the engagement on a company's page is from employees. If you want your strategy to win, make good use of employee advocacy. The employees want to see the brand succeed. Employees share content from their employers more than they do other types of content. And by the way, when information comes from an employee, people are more likely to trust it. 80% of LinkedIn users drive business decisions. The chief selling point of the platform is the ability to target people by their jobs, instead of just the demographics. A LinkedIn ad has the potential of reaching 12% of the earth's population (people over 13 years old). This percentage may not be the highest but at least the self-selected user-base is passionate about what they do. 30 million companies use LinkedIn. And they do not use it for recruiting only. Marketing and sales folks are on there too. LinkedIn is used by 94% of B2B marketers for content marketing. People are three times more likely to trust the content on LinkedIn compared to other platforms. So, this number is not surprising. LinkedIn is used by 89% of B2B marketers for lead generation. And according to 62% of these marketers, LinkedIn is effective for lead generation. 59% of sales professionals depend on social platforms to make sales. On average, Sponsored InMail sees a 52% open rate. LinkedIn's cost per lead is 28% lower than that of Google AdWords.

Chapter 19
The Ultimate Twitter Marketing Guide

You can find all the latest information you need about anything on Twitter. And this includes the latest updates from your favorite businesses and companies. Some businesses have managed to use Twitter to boost conversions, increase brand awareness, engage their customers and more. The platform attracts about 326 million monthly users from all over the world. You have an opportunity to share content with all of them. The idea of being able to reach all those people sounds interesting, doesn't it? But you should first ask yourself how you can create content that they will want to engage with. That is the point of this post. It is a comprehensive guide to Twitter marketing. A Twitter Marketing Strategy: What Is It? It is a plan for creating and sharing content with your followers, audience, and buyer personas on Twitter. Its purpose is to put your brand out there, attract new leads and boost sales. Forming a Twitter marketing strategy is just like creating a typical social media marketing strategy. The steps are the same: Research your target audience and buyer personas. Create great, interesting content. Schedule your posts. Analyze your results. What Is Unique About Twitter? There are several things that make Twitter a fantastic marketing tool. It is free. You can easily share branded content. It will expand your reach. It allows businesses to offer quick customer support. You can search your competitors to see their content and how they are doing it. Prospects can search for your business and learn more about it. You can communicate with your followers and share new updates with them. How Can You Use Twitter for Business? As you use Twitter for marketing, it is important that you reach the people you are targeting. Here are some steps you can follow to help with that. You can tweak them to suit your business. You want people to know that it is your businesses when they take a glance at the profile. Let it include your colors, logos and any memorable details that are associated with your brand. Handle: this is your Twitter username. Make sure it includes your business's name to make it easy for people to find you. Header: this is like the background image. You can use a branded image, your logo or just a unique image. Profile picture: this the picture that represents your business with every interaction, tweet, post, etc. You can use the CEO's photo, business initials, or your logo. Bio: this lets people know what the Twitter account is all about. You can write a brief description of the company, the mission statement or just something funny and engaging. Website URL: under the bio, there is a place for your URL. It will help direct traffic to your site. Birthday: input the date that the business was started to give your audience a little more information. Every Twitter user can create and view a list. It is a group of Twitter accounts that you have selected and organized in categories. Your lists could be for top marketing experts, leadership experts, etc. Opening a list displays the accounts' tweets only. Twitter lists allow you to follow specific handles. Feel free to segment the lists into groups: target audience, competitors, business inspiration, etc. You will be able to conveniently review their content, interactions, and posts. A Twitter chat could be for discussing a specific topic, engaging followers, asking for opinions about something from your audience or fostering a community. To host a TweetChat, set a date and time for the chat, pick a topic, and come up with a hashtag. Share the information on your bio, website or in a tweet. When someone wants to see the comments, questions, and responses regarding the topic, they can search the hashtag. Twitter Chats boost engagement and create a conversation around your brand. Advertising is an amazing way to quickly reach your target audience. Your tweets will be discovered by thousands of Twitter users and increase your influence. This is done through Twitter ads or promoted tweets. Promoted tweets: this feature displays your tweets in Twitter search results or Twitter streams to certain users. You will be charged a monthly fee. Twitter users can engage with these promoted tweets just as they would with organic content. Twitter Ads: the feature allows you to choose from various objectives including website conversions, video views and app installs. Whatever you pick determines the price you will pay. How can you increase your website traffic using Twitter? Include the business URL under your bio. Incorporate the URL in your tweets. Retweet other users' content that has links to your site. Embed tweets on your site using a Twitter Timeline. Drive traffic to a specific page using Twitter Ads. These are tweet collections about a certain even or topic. Create your own Moments so your followers can view them on your profile. Organize the Moments into categories so you can market events, industry news and campaigns related to your business. Apply for Twitter verification. You will get a blue checkmark badge once your application is accepted. It shows that your account is authentic. Your followers will not be confused or duped by accounts that try to impersonate your business. With more Twitter followers you will have more people interacting with what you post. You will get more website traffic and increase your brand awareness. How can you get more followers? Create shareable content. Use uncommon hashtags. Come up with engaging content: surveys, questions, contests, giveaways, etc. Work with Twitter influencers. Link to your Twitter account on your website. Engage your current followers. They will return the favor. You can use Search and Timeline keyword targeting to reach the relevant audience. Search keyword targeting: your tweets will be shown when users search for topics related to your brand. Timeline keyword targeting you can act on Twitter users' feelings based on what they tweet. People on Twitter are two times more likely to engage with tweets that have hashtags. Hashtags will expand your influence. But there are some rules that you should stick to. Create unique hashtags for your business. Let the hashtags be memorable and relevant. See which of your hashtags are successful (use Twitter Analytics). Avoid overusing hashtags. You do not make your tweets to look spammy. You need to tweet regularly to show consistency and give your followers content to engage with. And know the right time to post. According to research, these are the best times to tweet for businesses: 8 to 10 AM and 6 to 9 PM when users are commuting on weekdays. Noon and 5 to 6 PM all week. Weekends are the best days for B2Cs. Weekdays are the best days for B2Bs. After determining the best times to post, use a social media management tool to schedule the tweets. Some of the popular ones include: HubSpot, Twitter Analytics, and Sprout Social. Social media marketing campaigns help you increase traffic, drive sales, and reach your target audience. These are the steps to follow: Research the competition. Know how to capture the attention of your target audience. Decide what content to create. Share the content and promote it. Monitor the results. Writing a strong bio is the first thing any visitor to your profile will read. Let it show them what they should expect. You only get 160 characters so make every word count. Your tweets should not just be all text. Include quality photos and videos. Visual content is eye-catching and prompts users to engage with your content. If you want followers to keep coming back, engage with them. It feels personal and fosters a sense of loyalty. "Like" interactions or tweet back.

Share images, URLs, videos, or articles anytime the media mentions your business. People will find it easier to trust your business. Follow the accounts or search their handles and see what they tweet. Check their response, comment, and retweet count. It is a great way to know whether their strategies are working or not. Focus on the Needs and Interests of Your Followers - When you fulfill their needs, they will find it easier to interact with your content. Study them to see what content they like. Create surveys or just ask them in your tweets. If you have a contest, giveaway or launch party coming up, schedule tweets or use a unique hashtag to promote it. This gives people an opportunity to know how they can participate. Users on Twitter can message you privately with concerns or questions. Let your business be known for prompt and efficient customer support by checking the inbox regularly. Analytics is important to check whether your efforts are bearing any fruit. Which metrics should you track? Engagement: analyze your tweets' click-throughs, favorites, replies, follows, and retweets. Impressions: this shows how many times your posts were shown on audience timelines. Hashtags: it shows your most used hashtags by followers and your audience. Top tweets: see which of your tweets have the most engagement. Contributors: analyze how your contributors' tweets are doing. Twitter Analytics is the best tool for checking your analytics. It is free and created specifically for Twitter. Anyone on the platform can use it. If you like, you can also incorporate Twitter Ads data.

Conclusion

I f your business has an online presence, you should aim at having a strong engagement. It is proof that the impact of your business is being felt in the market.

Not only does it increase popularity, but it also nurtures meaningful connections and may boost your ROI. What Is Social Media Engagement? It is the number of shares, likes, and comments. A big following is great, but an engaged audience is better than a big one—quality over quantity. There are certain metrics used to measure social media engagement. They include: Use of branded hashtags. Mentions. Click-throughs. Audience and followers' growth. Likes. Comments. Retweets/shares. Your followers can naturally start engaging with your content. But often, you may need to encourage them a little. Here are a few tricks to help you with that. Assess your engagement: see how many followers you have, the average number of shares and comments you get on each post and any other relevant numbers. Make sure you continue monitoring these numbers. Choose your strategy: every company has different goals and strategies are, thus, different. Your strategy will depend on your goals. This could be educating the audience, collecting feedback, changing the public perception, etc. Understand your audience: it is not easy to engage people you do not know. Seek to learn what resources, tone and type of language will work for them. Post valuable content: think more in terms of conversation and not broadcast. Stay topical: you do not always have to post new content every day. You can join in conversations. Comment on current trends and events. Do not forget to have fun with viral memes too. Keep the conversation going: incorporate both proactive and reactive engagement. Reactive engagement involves responding to comments, mentions and messages. Proactive engagement involves sparking conversation. Your human side: you may have noticed that brands' social teams usually sign off personally on posts. Show behind the scenes videos and photos. It helps to respond with warmth and humor too. Respond in time: answer questions as they come. You could even have an automated response for instant replies. Schedule properly: use a scheduling tool like Hootsuite to ensure that you post consistently and at the right times. Beyond the feed: in addition to engaging your audience on the feed, also consider story interactions and direct messages. Social Media Engagement Tools involves, Photo editing: crop pictures, add text and try different filters. Video editing: video is way more engaging that text or image. GIFs: these have become a huge part of communication on the internet. Analytics: you need a tool that will help you monitor your progress as far as social media engagement is concerned. After doing all that work, you will want to see whether you are making a difference. That is where social media analytics come in. There are tons of tools that will give you an overview of your numbers. Social platforms also offer a way for you to check your engagement.

www.ingramcontent.com/pod-product-compliance
Lightning Source LLC
Chambersburg PA
CBHW071235170526
45165CB00003B/1104